# Staying Married and Loving It!

Dr. Patricia Allen

# Staying Married and Loving It!

Dr. Patricia Allen

Copyright 2025 by Dr. Patricia Allen

All rights reserved. No part of this publication may be reproduced, stored in a retrieval system or transmitted in any form or by any means, electronic, mechanical, photocopying, recording or otherwise without the written permission of the Publisher.

First Printing 2025

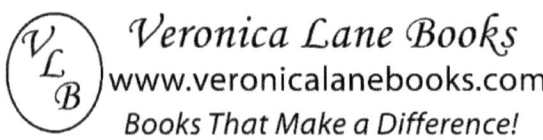

www.VeronicaLaneBooks.com :
Etan@VeronicaLaneBooks.com
11420 US-1, Ste 124, N. Palm Beach, FL 33408 USA
Tel: +1 (833) VLBOOKS +1 (833) 852-6657)

Library of Congress Cataloging-In-Publication Data

Allen, Patricia, 1936 -
Staying Married and Loving It! / by Dr. Patricia Allen

SUMMARY: The author presents various methods that couples can use to create a happy and equitable relationship.

ISBN: 979-8-34933-677-5

# Foreword

Before meeting Dr. Pat Allen, I was on a long-term search for personal growth and transformation. My professional studies began at the University of Southern California and then continued at the School of Natural Healing. In 1980, I created and ran a holistic wellness practice in Los Angeles.

My life morphed into a new phase of personal exploration after a series of devastating personal losses. I was fortunate enough to meet Dr. Pat Allen in 1994, just when her first bestseller *Getting to I Do* was published. A friend took me to see Dr. Allen at her regular Monday night relationship seminar in West Los Angeles. I immediately connected with her energy and loved her wit and intellect. I loved the way Dr. Allen was able to deliver a barrage of scientific information supporting her work in improving communication between couples. And she always brought along her own twist of sharp humor. Dr. Allen's wealth of knowledge and her powerful messaging was why I immediately knew that I wanted to deepen my studies at her side.

During the ensuing years, eventually collaborating with Dr. Allen as I developed more of my own dream analyst and Transactional Analyst work, I found that when she appeared in my dreams, it not only corroborated our close mentoring relationship but that my inner wisdom path was also accelerated.

I studied psychology and related physiology with Dr. Allen at her small private Los Angeles groups and at the Want Institute™ in Orange County. The Want Institute™ became my sanctuary, a deep well for crucial life information that I never had access to before. This gold mine of infinite possibilities pulled me further along my continuing quest into the wellness sciences. I began to see the connectivity between ancient wisdom and modern thought. I was able to open up hidden facets within myself, many times unpleasant. I had been operating in an out-of-balance, self-destructive manner that affected my relationships. Dr. Allen inspired me to systemically dump all of the old, distressing parts of my *script*, the downloads that we are all subjected to early on in our lives due to our DNA, parents, schools, church, peers, and media. Working with Dr. Allen,

I knew that I wanted to continue sharing my discoveries and gifts with others.

*Staying Married and Loving It*, Dr. Pat's second best-selling book, is based on her very special wisdom and guidance for happiness and longevity in relationships. This wisdom is built upon a foundation of mutual respect, clear communication, and understanding of the inherent differences between men and women in their emotional and psychological makeup. According to Dr. Pat, men thrive on respect and appreciation, while women seek love and security. By recognizing and honoring these needs, couples can create a stronger and longer-lasting bond.

Effective communication in an open, honest, and respectful dialogue between partners involves not only expressing one's own needs and desires but also actively listening to and understanding the partner's perspective. Couples need to set aside regular time to talk about their relationship, addressing any issues before they escalate to negativity. These methods establish clear boundaries to help protect individual autonomy and prevent resentment from building up, which helps maintain a healthy balance between togetherness and individuality.

Dr. Pat teaches that taking responsibility for one's own emotions is essential to a successful marriage, partnership, or any relationship. Instead of blaming the partner for negative feelings, she encourages individuals to explore their own emotional responses and work towards self-improvement. This approach fosters personal growth and reduces conflicts within the relationship.

A shared vision for the future is a cornerstone of Dr. Pat's philosophy. She advises couples to discuss and align their long-term goals, whether related to finances, family, or personal aspirations, thereby strengthening common partnership objectives and creating a sense of unity.

Finally, Dr. Allen emphasizes the importance of unwavering commitment and devotion not to the individual but to the relationship. She believes that a successful marriage requires consistent effort, patience, and a willingness to work through challenges together. By maintaining a steadfast commitment to the relationship, couples can build a lasting and fulfilling marriage or partnership.

By incorporating these principles into their relationships, couples will achieve lasting love and happiness. Enjoy this classic work. Read and re-read it until you master the proven techniques that have worked for thousands of couples whom Dr. Pat Allen has counselled for over 60 years.

Patrica Eltinge,<br>
Juno Beach, FL

# PREFACE

In 1974, I was a wife, mother of four, and junior high school art teacher, nearly one hundred pounds overweight. Then I read The Feminine Mystique, and my life changed. I lost weight, became a feminist, and went back to school to become a marriage counselor. My husband, a high school football coach who married me when I was totally dependent on him, didn't like my becoming his equal, and soon left me and our four daughters.

After my divorce, I immersed myself in the study of human behavior. I compiled data, working toward my psychotherapist's license. I listened, and I learned from the hundreds of couples I saw professionally. What I observed was that, in relationships, as women grew stronger and more male, men became intimidated and more female, reluctant to make a commitment to an independent woman who could leave them at will. These men still wanted a traditional, controllable, docile woman, not a "women's libber." Instead of leading to love, equality seemed to bring on conflict and confusion.

My professional goal was to learn whether a woman really could combine a career and marriage. How much independence and responsibility is good or bad in an intimate relationship? To come to terms with all the complexities of a contemporary relationship, I had to understand and then address the androgynous nature in all of us.

To validate my hunches, I went back to Carl Jung, the Swiss analyst who believed that each man and woman carried not only some hormones but also personality characteristics of the opposite sex. Using Jung's theories as a basis for my doctoral dissertation, I developed a theory that I call Androgynous Semantic Realignment. I also developed a strategy of accommodation to help men and women balance their feminine and masculine sides in an equitable exchange, without conflict, allowing them to share their gifts equitably as a couple.

In this strategy, known as WANT® Training, each person learns to retain both halves of his or her "wholeness." At the same time, each must subordinate his or her less dominant, or secondary, self by choosing to become either the respected leader (male) in the relationship or marriage, or the cherished follower (female), but not both.

Freud said, "Anatomy is destiny," and to some degree he was right. In a heterosexual couple, neurology, biology, and physical structure do help us in selecting the male or female role with greater ease than in a same-sex relationship. But the goals of a gay or lesbian couple are really no different from a heterosexual couple. Everyone wants to love and be loved.

Where nature supports similarity, as in same-sex couples, the mind must override the similarity and compensate through language. My communication technique, which I call Androgynous Semantic Realignment, or WANT® Training, is for everyone, straight or gay or lesbian. If both partners can move flexibly between their masculine, mental, money-making side and their feminine, physical, and feeling side, they are an "ambisexual, "androgynous," "narcissistically" healthy couple. They are able to choose from moment to moment which energy to express while being aware that the expression must complement and not compete with the energy of the other.

Please don't confuse what we are saying with the old-fashioned notion that a woman should be subservient to a man. On the contrary, people who choose the masculine energy must learn to temper their lead with an empathy for the feminine energy of their partners, who themselves must learn to balance their love for their partner with the responsibility to say no to things immoral or unethical.

"If it doesn't feel good, don't do it," whether it's the marriage bed, the cash register, the baby bassinet, the casting couch, or the boardroom couch. Sexual harassment doesn't have a place in the home or the office.

I want to teach you to say "No!" to being manipulated through intimidation or seduction into becoming a usable, abusable mother figure to your husband or children. The idea that a woman's real job is to see others grow and accomplish things in their lives, while she reaps her reward by basking in their glow, is not acceptable to me. Mothering is a terminal illness when given to able-bodied people over the age of ten.

It is my goal to teach you to be a woman who can say no to a husband who spends money on his toys at the expense of your training class and babysitter, or to children who demand expensive designer clothes, at the cost of your own development or wardrobe. I want you to learn to say no to bosses who demand mothering in the form of little extras, such as overtime necessitated by poor management or homemaking with food, drink, or cleaning outside of your job specifications. It's important for you to say no to anyone who projects "mother" onto you and limits you in any way you haven't chosen for yourself, and especially to say no to religious, cultural, or ethnic groups who say mothering is a woman's highest calling. The highest calling of a woman or man is to be her or his total self, a sensuous sexual partner, and a nurturing human being with a good career. Negotiating for mutual benefit and not being intimidated or seduced by narcissistic men and women is my goal for you.

From a vantage point of twenty-five years, I see the results of my professional work in the thousands of women and men who attend my seminars, and experiment and explore and learn. They become more skilled in loving and relating. More than five thousand couples are now in happy, loving marriages and committed relationships through the use of my techniques.

It happened to me, too. One evening, a very delightful man came to one of my seminars. He kept coming back, and we got to know each other. Over the next three years, he used what he learned to court me. In 1990, I married Guy, my masculine man.

In my first book, *Getting to I Do,* I showed you how to choose your masculine or feminine energy, find a complementary man, attract him to you, begin a healthy sexual relationship, and get married, or at least engaged, by the end of the first year. The biggest impact of the book has been the word-of-mouth message passed on to already married couples by single women and men who have used my communication techniques. Hundreds have contacted me for marriage and family therapy based on the first book. With this, my new book, we can continue to go deeper into helping to foster long-lasting and happy relationships.

My special thanks go to the thousands of women and men who have, through their successes and failures, helped me learn each idea, and each technique, every step of the way. This book is a result of twenty-five years of research with thousands of women just like me. Because of their wish to enhance their ability to be happily married, they helped me compile the information that forms this book. As a therapist and a woman, I owe much to these clients and students.

And finally, I thank you, the reader. As long as women (and men) like you pursue better answers for life's concerns through books, seminars, and lectures, the human race will profit by better marriages and families.

This book is for any couple who is trying to stay together into their golden years. It is addressed to women and men who are in a marriage or committed relationship but are having problems because of confusion and competition. Much of the book reflects upon the same framework and principles of *Getting to I Do* with a few case histories that apply here as well. I have taken the liberty of restating their importance in this book. *Staying Married and Loving It* teaches my unique techniques for marital and relationship happiness that couples can apply on their own according to their individual needs and wants.

Because mine is a new and different way of looking at relationships, my rules of behavior may anger some people. But I can't help that; the rules work. My system is not complex, but it does answer the needs of individuals who live in a complex world. To be unique, individuated, actualized women and men, we each must achieve a healthy egocentric-but not egotistic-narcissism. What I advocate is that you make educated choices in your life, relationships, and career.

We each must choose a style of life. If you want to be a single entrepreneur, then, like a golfer, you need not be on a team to win. However, if you want to be in a successful, romantic, committed relationship, then you must choose to be like a baseball player who needs to consider their teammates.

You decide which is right for you.

Dr. Patricia Allen
Newport Beach, California

# Contents

| | |
|---|---|
| Foreword | 5 |
| Preface | 8 |

## Part One: What's Wrong And How To Make It Right

| | |
|---|---|
| Why People Aren't Staying Married | 14 |
| Choose to Be the Masculine or Feminine-Energy | 20 |
| Respect or Cherish | 31 |
| Three Styles of Marriage | 50 |

## Part Two: Staying Married 21

| | |
|---|---|
| How to Communicate with Love | 61 |
| How to Have Great Sex | 93 |
| How to Deal with Money | 116 |
| Dysfunctional Families: Problems with Friends and Children | 127 |
| Switching Roles | 142 |
| Addictions and Obsessions | 150 |
| Midlife: When Men Become Women and Women Become Men | 171 |

## Part Three: When Nothing Works

| | |
|---|---|
| Separation | 191 |
| Divorce | 200 |

## Part Four: The Rest of the Story

| | |
|---|---|
| Widows and Widowers | 209 |
| Ten Secrets to Staying Married | 212 |

# Part One

# What's Wrong and How to Make It Right

# Why People Aren't Staying Married

In the old days, men were men and women were women, but this is no longer true. Today we have multiple choices, and we need new concepts if we are to mate and marry and stay married. With poor role modeling by divorced parents and conflicting media images of maleness and femaleness, men and women are creating a mixture of old traditions and new-age values to the confusion of everyone. Western culture has traditionally cast men as the protectors, leaders, and predominant doers. Men have traditionally proposed to women, have conferred status upon women, and have been the security providers. Women, on the other hand, have been the domesticators, the followers, the recipients- they have made themselves available to the life plans of men and have been responsive to male needs. Maleness, in this scheme, is the pragmatic, functional way in which we handle work and initiate action. It is verbal, centered in the left lobe of the brain. Femaleness is the passive, the receptive, the emotional centered in the right lobe of the brain; it can be represented as nonverbal energy. Its function in traditional terms is to serve as an outlet for emotion and a moral brake; it can be represented as non-verbal energy. Its function in traditional terms is to serve as an outlet for emotion and a moral brake; it can be seen as the stable center that allows a relationship to develop and be maintained.

Although both male and female elements are vital to the makeup of both men and women, for a relationship to be healthy and successful, they must be reconciled and be complementary. In other words, there can only be one male and one female in every relationship.

Marriage has become a unique problem in this day and age because no one needs to be married anymore. This is partly because we have all become complex ambisexual human beings who have totally new and diverse choices in career and love. (Ambisexuality means that every man has female aspects, and every woman has male aspects.) Of course, people have always been ambisexual, but in the past, limitations on their choices seemed helpful for society. Rigid roles for men and women forced men to repress their feminine side and women their masculine side.

In those days, churches, ethnic groups, and cultures ordered us to behave in certain ways. That is, men, with penises, shall give to, protect, and cherish people without penises! Women, without penises, shall passively wait for and respond to men.

Those were the rules. Men wanted women for sex and housekeeping skills and women were grateful to have a man marry them and take care of their financial needs. Women who didn't marry or had to support themselves were forced to take low-paying, go-nowhere jobs such as typists, waitresses, factory workers, or other designated women's work.

Then, in the early 1970s, the feminist movement burst on the scene. For the first time "maleness," or the male qualities that represented success, was something that could be actively pursued by women. Money, power, independence, and prestige were all within a woman's grasp, and for the first time represented something that could be realistically achieved without sacrificing cultural values. Sacrificed instead were the traditional male and female roles that for generations had been the foundation of successful relationships. In fact, women became ashamed, and understandably so, given their new acculturation of being satisfied with the traditional female role.

No longer happy to be housewives, typists, or teachers, women now took on roles formerly considered masculine. They became managers, lawyers, college professors, and corporation presidents. They took assertiveness courses, had casual sex, acquired "boy toys" and gold credit cards, left their husbands, and went to sperm banks, at the same time that men were releasing a more loving, gentle, and sensitive side of their nature-nurturing children, crying openly, and using blow dryers. In Jungian terms, both women and men had begun to develop the "other" side of their true selves— the masculine as well as the feminine.

Soon, there were no rules of behavior particular to the male or the female in a romantic relationship. He could call her or she could call him. Either one could pay for the date, or they could split it. She could initiate sex, or he could. In both courting and marriage, equality became the name of the game. He fought for his opinions, and she fought for hers. He wanted to have his feelings taken care of, and so did she. The problem was that instead of two people in a graceful dance of give and take, marriage became a kind of battleground on which men and women sought equal status and equal degrees of power and prestige. With both men and women vying for the same position, the dance was abandoned as two partners struggled for the lead. In the process, we forgot how to make love to one another.

So why do people still want to get married? For the benefits of marriage, which include love, companionship, family stability, shared parenthood, career support, spiritual nourishment, and the status of Mr. and Mrs.

But grim statistics tell us that half the marriages performed today are doomed to end in divorce. More people are single than married and more kids than ever are now in single-parent homes. Teams are not making it anymore and our world shows the results, especially in our children's lives.

This book is a team training manual. It teaches highly evolved human beings over the age of twenty-five who don't need marriage but who want it to voluntarily give up their freedom as individuals. It also shows them that sharing their life with another equally evolved person is worth the price they pay in loss of some freedom.

But why must they voluntarily give up their freedom as individuals? Most marital problems occur when people try to maintain their single freedom and yet gain married benefits. The problem is narcissism, wanting it all.

Most marital problems occur when people try to maintain their single freedom and yet gain married benefits. The problem is narcissism-wanting it all. Narcissists don't give up any freedom: the Freedom to come and go as they please with whomever they choose; the freedom to control not only their life, money, sex, and time but yours as well.

There is nothing wrong with healthy narcissism. Becoming an independent, narcissistically healthy, actualized man or woman is good for everyone, but when marriage and family become a goal, narcissism disallows the realization of that goal.

We used to think that there was one man and one woman in every relationship, but now we know there are two men and two women because every person has both masculine and feminine energy. So in today's relationships, you're actually dealing with four people: the feminine energy of the woman and her masculine energy, and the masculine energy of a man and his feminine energy. This may sound like a crowded household, and it is, especially when everyone wants everything. It's four energy systems fighting for two places in bed. This means that when they both have the same needs or wants at the same time (and they will), a conflict in the form of a push-pull power play will occur. This neutralizes the sensitivity and the sexuality that a romantic relationship needs to flourish.

We know that in romance only opposites attract. People who are similar, if they come together, tend to repel. What is romance? It's a woman for example, fantasizing that a man cares so much about her that he'll be generous to her, he'll protect her, and he'll cherish her feelings ahead of his own. He acts like her man.

The other side of this romantic ideal is that a woman will listen to her man's ideas and defer to his thinking. She doesn't challenge him, make him prove himself, or make him feel inadequate. She lets him be respectable, lets him into her space, and receives from him-without bristling. She doesn't feel challenged and confronted just because he's telling her what he thinks she should do. She's not worried that if she doesn't have equality, she will lose power. She becomes his woman.

That is the tradeoff and big surprise—it works! It's equity instead of equality. One male and one female create a passionate team, which is a credit to both people's ability to set their egos aside for the sake of the covenant. Between them, all their needs are met and success is inevitable, barring outside catastrophes. Even in the face of a catastrophe, the team will regroup and continue to go forward because they can communicate through the turmoil and confusion.

This has nothing to do with subservience but, on the contrary, a wholly new way for men and women to relate. Our ideas are not anti-feminist but liberating. Be what you want to be. But take it one step further. The principles of *Staying Married and Loving It* go beyond feminism to embrace an even more modern and liberated approach to women's issues and marriage.

Believe me, the husband who believes in the traditional marriage where he gets to be king of the hill and his wife the dependent doormat who lets him get away with it will be in for a rude awakening when he finds out that she has either left him or is having an affair out of resentment.

If you are bound to cliches such as "Share your feelings, thoughts, needs, so you both feel loved," or "Men are born leaders, women born nurturers," or "Today's men are so sensitive they need respectable women to take charge," or "Today's liberated women need to be kept in line by tough guys who can handle them," you will hate this book. Instead, why not open your mind and heart to a new twenty-first-century way of relating that supports every part of everyone—body, mind, and soul.

*Staying Married and Loving It!* offers new choices to any man or woman who wishes to achieve a stable marriage or long-term relationship. It's a manual for how to sacrifice without degradation and resentment. It's a book that will help healthy narcissists become great team members.

Freud, at the end of his career, asked the question, "What do women want?" The most common answer today is "Everything," and that is exactly what's wrong. Women and men who want it all, end up with nobody to love.

## Does This Sound Like You?

You're attractive, successful, liberated, and complex. You've got a great job, a terrific house or apartment, and you're in a marriage or committed relationship. Maybe you've got a couple of kids. You're a woman other women are jealous of because you've got it all.

So why do you find yourself envying couples you see on the street, holding hands and smiling at each other? How come your love life has turned from a thrilling adventure into simple sex without much affection?

It's not too late to turn your marriage around. I'll show you the clues you've missed and why. I'll also show you how to bring back the passion you once knew, using my principles that work rather than yours that don't.

Perhaps you're sitting home alone again, while he's working long hours, or out with the guys or another woman.

I can teach you to get his attention, talk about the problem, and solve it. I'll give you ten secrets that will allow you to waltz as a team rather than slam dance as competitive narcissists heading for divorce.

I know you really don't want to lose one another. Inside, you're hurt and angry. You love him, and he loves you. You desperately want to make the relationship work, but you're frightened that the constant collisions and unspoken secrets are tearing you apart. And you're right, they will—If you don't do something soon!

Maybe it's you who stays late at the office, fighting for a promotion, while he's being Mr. Mom with the house and kids. In that case, you'll have to decide whether to leave your power plays at the office or take them home and play hardball with your mate. I'll teach you how to make the right choice for you.

Or maybe you're going the other way, trying to become a Martha Stewart clone, hoping that a gourmet dinner and the perfect flower arrangement will bring back the magic but of course, it never does.

You fantasize about a new life alone with someone better suited to your needs, but what about the kids? What about money? What about going back to the meat market in the age of AIDS?

It's not too late, even if you've tried everything: therapy, church counseling, all the self-help groups, or keeping it all inside. I'll show you the path the two of you must walk to maintain openness, intimacy, love, and passion.

# Choose to Be the Masculine or Feminine-energy

It is my theory that in order to make a marriage work, each person must decide freely whether to be the masculine-energy partner or the feminine-energy partner. Neither partner can be both. Today, we all have access to both energies, active masculine and passive feminine, so we need inner choice. We cannot chaotically or spontaneously jump back and forth between the two. That destroys relationships and wears down one or both partners.

It doesn't matter whether it's the man or the woman who chooses to be the masculine energy or the feminine energy, as long as there is only one of each. If a woman chooses to be the feminine-energy partner, she should marry a masculine-energy man. If, however, a woman chooses to be the masculine-energy partner, she must be certain that her husband wants to be the feminine-energy partner, because if not, she will collide with her masculine man. Your goal is to make a clear decision about your energy before you begin a relationship, if you can. If that hasn't happened, you must negotiate for better results once you are in the marriage..

Of course, once you've chosen your primary role, you don't have to stick with it forever. As a married or committed couple, you can add variety for spice. You may go from masculine giving to feminine receiving. This is fine too, as long as you negotiate these changes with your partner and courteously switch styles.

I believe that marriage is an equitable barter of sex for money, with each partner sharing the responsibility for each other's need to be adequate providers and desirable lovers. The person who chooses to be the masculine-energy is the primary provider, the generous and protecting partner who brings status and security and is in charge of the material side of the relationship, money, property, and work. He (it is usually, but not always, he) sacrifices his natural, God-given right to be irresponsible, polygamous, and spoiled, in order to lead the team toward their mutually negotiated goals.

The person who chooses to be the feminine energy is the sensual and sexual partner, who is receptive, responsive, and available to a masculine partner. She (it is usually, but not always, she) sacrifices her hard-earned, liberated right to be independent, to initiate, to be respected, and to co-lead in order to follow her man and serve on his team. The male initiates and the female follows, but with the absolute right to veto anything unethical or immoral as well as anything that doesn't feel good to her body or hurts her money, property, or career.

A woman can be the masculine energy without castrating a man or be the feminine energy without denying her own personality. We now have the freedom and ability to choose whether we want to be the masculine or feminine energy, and while hormones, brain differences, language patterns, and temperament may direct us toward certain choices, we must finally be guided by what feels most natural to us. Each of us must look inside ourselves, examine our real desires and feelings, and act on them. Now, we can attain any type of romantic relationship we desire, not based on our genitals, but on who we really are.

The biggest message of this book is "Make your choice and go for it with gusto." Because we are of the twenty-first century, we are bisexual, narcissistic, and androgynous, we have more choices of behavior than ever before. The slaves are freed. What do we do with the freedom?

## What About Anatomy and Hormones?

Although the social-sexual revolution freed us to be either the masculine or feminine energy in a relationship, hormones play a major role in shaping our choices. Gender contributes powerfully to our energy preferences, with most women still wanting to be the feminine energy and most men the masculine energy.

Because of the female hormone estrogen, most women under the age of fifty fall into being the feminine energy. Estrogen is a feeling hormone, which means that the feminine energy of a woman's primary interest (despite the need to earn a living) will be emotions and relationships. The ultimate feminine desire is to make love because it is the closest and most intimate thing that two people can do.

Women need to feel good to do well. A woman influenced by estrogen processes her feelings and thoughts so she can decide to move toward pleasure if she feels good or stop the action if she feels bad. The female principle is "I feel and I don't want pain." Processing allows a woman to continually track her feelings and then act on them.

Because of the male hormone testosterone, a man under fifty will be driven to doing and will prefer to be the masculine-energy. Testosterone is an action hormone that leads men toward performance, power, money, and sex. This translates into most men being interested in buying, selling, and building. Their world is concrete and performance-oriented.

The male principle is "I think and I want." Knowing what he thinks and wants allows a masculine-energy man to focus. A focused, thinking, masculine-energy man will act decisively, which will elicit respect from you, a feminine-energy woman.

Men need to do well to feel good. A young man who is influenced by his testosterone will want to produce, or perform a task, so that he can feel good about the result. Often, he'll perform for the intellectual pleasure of achieving his goals of money, power, and prestige. Of course, women perform too, but men's bodies are built more for performance than process.

For example, because of the way testosterone affects a man, he'll be less likely than a woman to experience discomfort working in an unesthetic environment. This is because he can focus on the task at hand with less sensitivity to people and things around him. What is seen as insensitivity by his woman is seen by the man as efficient, effective, and economical.

However, as time goes by, we see a reversal as nature pushes us toward our opposite energy. In midlife, we swap roles. The energy of men becomes more passively feminine. Their testosterone lowers, making them less aggressive and more receptive as the estrogen in their bodies promotes sensitivity and feeling. The energy of women, however, becomes more actively masculine after menopause, when their estrogen level drops and progesterone impacts them more. Often, this is the point at which women go out into the money world to make their mark while men are ready to retire to their homes and pleasures such as cooking, gardening, art, or music.

Men who manage midlife well become more receptive to the nurturing and sensual (feminine) aspects of themselves, while women who thrive in midlife become more assertive and autonomous (masculine). Couples must at this point renegotiate their roles equitably and voluntarily, with pride and ego set aside.

## Brain Differences Between Men and Women

Part of the male-female communication problem is that the thought processes for men and women are different. Everyone's brain has two lobes. The left lobe is the thinking, active, concrete, masculine lobe, and the right lobe is feeling-centered, nonverbal, receptive, and feminine. Between these is a fibrous mass called the corpus callosum, which receives information from and links both lobes. Because this tissue is smaller in right-handed men than it is in left-handed men or in women, right-handed men generally act from either their left lobe (teaching, verbalizing, problem solving), or their right lobe (sensuous, nonverbal, sexual), but rarely from both right and left lobes at the same time.

A woman, however, because her corpus callosum is larger, is capable of processing data from both her right and left lobes at the same time, in effect melding her thoughts and feelings. This can cause problems in a relationship between a woman and a right-handed man when she expects him to be able to speak freely about feelings, and he expects her to be logical. Often, a right-handed man is confused about his bright, sensitive woman, and says, "How can anyone be so smart and so dumb at the same time?"

When Terry, a policeman, surprised his wife, Lilly, a bookkeeper, by taking her to a small airfield for a jaunt in a twin-engine plane, he was amazed and irritated by her terrified reaction. How could Lilly be so illogical? he wondered. A twin-engine plane was a lot safer than a jumbo jet. At least if anything went wrong, there was a chance of the plane gliding to the ground. How could Lilly handle her job if she were so illogically emotional about this issue of flying? He couldn't help making disparaging remarks.

But Lilly wanted Terry's understanding that the flight was a problem for her, logical or not. She didn't want his ridicule. Collisions between Terry's logical and Lilly's illogical reactions had been a chronic problem until they heard me speak on neurological differences between women and right-handed men.

By realizing that there was actually a biological difference in their brains, Terry was able to empathize with Lilly's feelings and give her cherishing comfort, which eventually helped her desensitize her to fear. It is important to realize that empathy in itself can have a healing effect on the other person. Expressing empathy offers support while your partner works out her or his inner conflicts.

Kent, 53, had to travel every month as a district manager for an automotive parts distributorship. Each time he left Candace, 50, at home, she told him he didn't have to call nightly. If he listened to her and didn't call every night, when he got home he'd invariably find her upset. She'd mutter about how he couldn't call her because he was probably too busy entertaining a young bimbo.

I told him that he was dealing with the complexities of a woman's way of thinking. A woman can meld two themes into one blur, thinking "He's a busy man. I'm a grown-up woman, I don't need him to call," and at the same time "I'm a sensitive female who misses my husband and likes receiving calls that aren't practical or necessary, but loving and reassuring."

Confusion reigns. Her mouth says, "Don't call," but her heart says, "Do call." A man can be caught in a logical masculine bind. To decide what to do, he must determine whether his primary energy is masculine or feminine. Then, he needs either to respect her logical statement, "You don't have to call," or to understand that no matter what she says, she wants him to cherish her by calling.

Facts, especially for a woman or a left-handed or an older man, are colored by feelings and emotions. Right-handed men and older women can perceive reality more objectively than younger women or left-handed men. The corpus callosum also allows a woman to pick up intuitive perceptive messages from situations that are not subject to logic, so she can follow her husband into places where sheer logic would tell her not to go. But it also makes her flexible and capable of being conned or manipulated and led.

Of course, left-handed men can speak logically and with feelings, as a woman can. This can be terrific for a woman, because talking to such a man can be like talking to your best friend. Yet sometimes, all hell can break loose, because you both have a lot of emotion behind your thoughts and don't want to compromise.

If you and your left-handed mate both have had a difficult day at work and feel distraught and maybe a little depressed when you get together at night, you may find that because both of your needs for comfort are so acute, neither of you will be able to console the other person. This could easily result in resentment, anger, verbal attacks, or a withdrawal of affection. Therefore, if your husband is left-handed, it's important that you and he decide early in the marriage or relationship, which of you will be respected for logic and which will be cherished for your feelings. You both must override your natural ability to think and feel at the same time.

There is a distinction between actions influenced by physical reality such as hormones or anatomy and actions that are a result of a psychological dysfunction, as when a stalemate occurs because both want their feelings cherished at the same time. A constant collision, male versus male or female versus female, will undermine the natural flow of intimacy. A death grip can ensue, which can end in violence or the end of the marriage.

## How Men Fall In Love And How Women Share Love

Only a masculine man falls in love; a feminine woman doesn't. She must already love herself. If a woman has been well-loved by her father, she will love herself. Then, when a man proposes to her, she'll be able to consider what he can add to her life. If she can do better by herself, she'll say, "No thank you." But if he can add to her life, she simply shares with him the love she has for herself. And he'll make her life better for the sharing. Men fall in love by falling out of their logical, rational, insensitive heads into their hearts and bodies, where love can be felt, touched, and shared.

A man cannot fall in love with a woman who doesn't already love herself. A woman who loves a man more than she loves herself risks an addictive obsession in which she loses herself completely in the service of his narcissistic ego. This is, classically speaking, the woman who will do anything for a man.

A man projects a virtuous image on the woman he wants to marry. In the old days, our churches, our parents, and the rest of society ordered women to be virtuous, but when women got the pill, we rebelled. Our rebelliousness was appropriate, but not our loss of virtue, which even in these modern times turns men away from marriage. Men want to be married to women they can predict will not have sex with other men.

'The reason men fall in love with the ideal of a woman is that they have a natural craving to raise their own spiritual and emotional standards. First, his rite of passage from boyhood into manhood takes place when he stops seeing women, children, animals, and the planet as sources of personal gratification and instead sees them as recipients of his manful, loving bounty. Then, when he falls in love, he wishes and strives to be a better man. You hear the phrase "A man is a man until he meets a lady, then he becomes a gentleman." The lady sets a standard that requires him to become a gentleman and cherish her.

It's a woman's responsibility to raise a man's level of consciousness from the concrete level of money and sex, where he's comfortable, to the spiritual level of love and relationships, where she's comfortable. If a woman does this correctly, men will usually comply because they are logical thinkers. Whether they admit it or not, men want women to set the spiritual standard in the relationship. When a masculine-energy man marries, he puts his mind, body, heart, soul, and money into the commitment. He takes on the responsibility not only for his woman but for everybody she loves.

There is a kind of man, however, for whom falling in love is dangerous. This man will not usually risk falling in love more than once in his life, because if the relationship fails, he may lose confidence in all facets of his life, including business. He will then usually distrust women to such a degree that he'll swear never to fall in love again. This kind of man uses women for gratification.

# Oxytocin, the Love Hormone

Most modern, liberated, sexually active women believe they can maintain control over their emotions after making love. What they don't realize is that when a woman gives her body to a man, there's a strong chance that she's going to bond to him, even after only one good sexual encounter. This is due to a sexually stimulated hormone called oxytocin, which is predominant in females and triggers orgasm.

During sex, women produce higher levels of oxytocin than men do, and women need more oxytocin to achieve orgasm. Even worse, according to Dr. Marie Carmichael, of Stanford University, is that women who are sexually aroused by the taste, touch, sight, smell, and sound of a man can love that man addictively, while the man remains physically uncommitted. Breaking this kind of addiction can take up to two years.

Too often, a woman who is sexually bonded to her masculine-energy man will often go out of her way to give him another chance, or make excuses for him, or delay confronting him when his priorities have slipped into selfishness. This is a big mistake. As soon as you perceive your masculine-energy man is headed in that direction, you must talk to him about your negative feelings.

For this reason, a feminine-energy woman shouldn't rationalize away her feelings in favor of her husband's. For example, women who are with alcoholic or abusive men often say things like "Oh, he was abused as a child," or "He only does it once in a while." The result is that she cherishes destructive men, which is self-destructive for a woman.

Masculine-energy men do not bond through sex. They bond through the commitments they make and keep. Why don't masculine men get hooked on sex and bond the way women do? Be- cause bonding is created by the receiving of physical pleasure, and although oxytocin works the same way in men as in women, women both produce more oxytocin and seem to be more susceptible to its emotional effects. Another reason that assertive, dynamic men don't bond through sex is that they override their feminine, feeling-oriented aspects with logical, testosterone-based, action-oriented behavior.

Of course, there are men who do bond through sex. Predominantly, they are feminine-energy men, who are more right-lobe, feeling oriented; older men, whose testosterone is diminishing; left-handed men, who have more access to their feelings neurologically; and men who have been raised mostly by women and have learned about feelings from them.

## It's Your Choice

Usually, it's the masculine-energy partner who brings status and security to the relationship. But often, feminine-energy men use the sensitivity, creativity, and intuition that are a part of their energy to make a lot of money. They will own the best art galleries, hotels, and restaurants. As career professionals, they make the best doctors, writers, actors, artists, and teachers. Their feminine energy, along with their physical maleness, lends itself to good human-loving interaction; thus, money follows. But whatever his profession, your feminine-energy husband is a sensitive man who can offer sensuality and sexuality to a strong woman who will back up his career with her brains. In a world where men should be men and women should be women, these alternative lifestyle couples need to know that they are normal and healthy.

Some feminine-energy husbands don't have careers. They function best in areas where relationships are important, such as home, children, and romance. Some wives want a home and family and are willing to bring home the money and status to provide it. We must look inside ourselves, examine our real desires, and then act on them. Respecting and accepting men's choices to use their creativity in the home and their sensitivity in relationships is the only logical balance for the masculine-energy woman.

Feminine-energy men don't like to fight, but they do appreciate masculine women who like to compete, lead, provide, and generally take charge outside the relationship. Within the relationship, feminine-energy men feel respected when their feelings are cherished and masculine-energy women feel cherished when their ideas are respected. They complement each other's needs.

So ask yourself the question, "Am I a woman with a career or a career woman?" If you see yourself as a woman with a career, you will probably have to make some professional sacrifices to enhance your man's career prospects, such as giving up a great job and moving to another city because his promotion includes a relocation, or even giving up your career while you are raising the children, and then perhaps resuming the career later.

There is a time to put career ahead of womanhood, and there is a time to put womanhood ahead of career. The biggest mistake is trying to do both at the same time. I usually recommend that young women get ready for a big career after the age of 45, but prepare for womanhood early, but you have got to decide yourself, "What is my priority or family?" Once you've decided, act accordingly and marry a man who supports your choice.

Infertility hits hard on overstressed, ambitious, liberated women. Anxious, overachieving superwomen signal the brain that a war is ongoing or imminent. The brain responds by not releasing the natural tranquilizer serotonin. Because serotonin deprivation impacts the hormones necessary for fertility, these masculine-energy women are kept infertile to protect them from the burden of pregnancy and babies.

Married for five years with no pregnancies, Velma, 38, and Serge, 40, were preparing for in-vitro fertilization. She had heard that I had strong opinions about fertility and came to my seminar to hear me speak on the subject.

My advice to Velma and other women like her is that if you want families, get back into a more feminine, sensitive lifestyle. Women need to feel good to do well, including getting pregnant. Getting sucked up in the corporate structure like "one of the boys" may make you as infertile as one of the boys. Women's bodies must be cared for as sensitive, responsive mechanisms rather than as machines that override pain and fatigue. Thriving in a masculine-energy arena is not the highest goal of a woman who wishes to be fertile. Saying no to overwork and competition may be saying yes to marriage and having babies.

As a woman "performs" like a man, she strains her instinctive tendency to stop whatever is painful or stressful. When a woman processes like a sensitive woman, she watches for tiredness, sleep or eating problems, menstrual cycle malfunctioning, and stops what she is doing until her body feels better. Hopefully, she's married to a man who wants her to feel good to do well and supports her pulling back to rest and recoup. If he wants her to stay productive at work or at home, he'll gain some money but lose his woman and babies. In vitro fertilization can help mechanically, but how can a woman be a mother if she acts like a man? Are you a career woman or a woman with a career?

Performance and productivity are masculine energy, whether at work or at home. If you choose to be a woman with a career on the side, you must follow your leader husband in all areas of marriage, including child raising, home decorating, and finances.

Although you have the feeling veto, you are not the boss. If you pretend that you like being the little woman when you really want to run the show, however, you'll confuse both of you, become resentful, and spend your productive energy trying to control him and undermine his self-esteem. Women who try to control men out of fear of their own vulnerability to masculine potency attempt to castrate their men but end up paying for it as men learn to hate women's castrating power.

I'm often asked whether a masculine-energy woman can choose to become feminine and whether a career woman can change and become a woman with a career. The answer is yes, but if she does decide to change, she has to be able to receive a man's masculine leadership without rebelling against him, which isn't easy for a woman who has grown accustomed to her masculine energy.

If this is you, evaluate your real desires about being the strong leader or the devoted follower before you get married. Otherwise, you'll find yourself fighting your man for the throne. Remember, pretense has no place in relationships. Be grounded in self-awareness, confidence, and integrity.

# Respect or Cherish

Within the relationship, the feminine-energy woman will feel respected when her feelings are cherished, and her masculine-energy man will feel cherished when his thinking is respected.

The husband will earn respect from his wife by putting her feelings ahead of his own, even when this is clearly a compromise of his human right to have his feelings cherished also. The wife gets her husband to protect and cherish her by respecting his ideas, thoughts, and opinions, even though she may know better, as long as he is moral and ethical with her body and her money.

When a masculine-energy man cherishes a feminine-energy woman, he'll like giving more to her. He'll feel secure in knowing that she needs him and won't leave him. He'll like being her protector and caring for her. She'll in turn feel secure and therefore respectful and loving toward him, as he feels loving toward her.

For a woman, to be loved is to be accepted. To cherish a feminine-energy woman despite her behaving badly is the ultimate gift from a masculine-energy man. He's with her on her painful journey, even though there is little or nothing in it for him at that moment. But his reward will come later when in appreciation, the feminine-energy partner gives respect multiplied tenfold. She'll also accept leadership and work for team goals and give pleasure by safely opening up to him emotionally and sexually.

Feminine-energy women verbalize their painful feelings, and they need to know their men will accept them, even if disapprovingly. Masculine-energy men like to nurture their loved ones. Their own feminine aspect wishes to empathize and share. They aren't macho men out of touch with their feelings and unwilling to be open to another's pain. Instead, they're confident that they can cherish their woman until a solution for her problem can be found. They don't run away from her pain, nor do they expect her to handle it alone.

Sometimes, a testosterone-based, level-headed masculine man will be annoyed with his feminine wife at just the time she needs his cherishing because she's not as logical as he expects her to be. Often, the words she's screaming at the top of her lungs are meaningless, even though she thinks they are logical, and she's really saying, "I'm scared. I feel jealous. I feel sad. I feel confused." The difference between what she says and what she means often results in conflict, which can lead to the destruction of the relationship.

But what if the man didn't say a word but just hugged the woman, even though she was hostile? Lines of communication would remain open, she and her man could relax and reconnect with her smart self and talk rationally. For a masculine man to say, "Honey, I hear your pain, but I haven't got a clear idea what it's about. Could you talk more about it?" is heaven on earth for a feminine woman.

But suppose he doesn't? Jung believed that men's feminine side, their "anima," helped them either to love women or use them, just as women's masculine side, their "animus," helped them either to be strong and self-loving or angry and self-destructive. The anima of a man is far more sensitive than a woman's animus. When a broken, blue, angry woman, or one with PMS (which, to me, stands for "Permission to Murder his Soul"), uses any excuse to hurt a man's sensitive side, it's because she believes she needs to control him before he hurts her. When a broken man uses any excuse to insult and undermine a woman's potency, it's because he feels inadequate beside her and is afraid she will hurt him before he can cut her down to size.

If you choose to be the feminine energy, respecting your husband's thinking ahead of your own means that whether or not his ideas, desires, or opinions agree with yours, you must listen, revere, honor, esteem, and accept them, or negotiate a change (I will teach you how) so that he feels respected.

A masculine-energy man needs to be respected by his feminine-energy wife, so don't criticize his opinions, argue about his philosophies, teach him the right way to do things, belittle him, or fight for sexual control. Being a feminine, sensual female means you don't compete intellectually with your masculine-energy husband; you keep your mouth shut and let him do most of the talking.

Instead of advice, try offering him affection and respect. Be positive, supportive, and encouraging about his ideas, plans, and opinions. Say things like "Gee, you're nice," and "Thanks so much," and "I appreciate that." You must nourish your masculine-energy husband's self-esteem. Women who can't allow themselves to feel little next to their man are often afraid to be vulnerable and intimate. They believe they must feel equal to or even better than their man.

It is human nature to like to feel empowered. But unless you want to feel this way all the time and be the masculine-energy in the relationship, resist short-term temptations in favor of the high ground, long-range objective of a successful marriage with your masculine-energy husband. Accept that he may have a point of view worth hearing, then hear it and go with it, unless it's unethical or immoral, doesn't feel good to your body, or hurts your money, property, or career. Don't explain or defend your feelings. Instead, say, "I appreciate the idea, but I don't feel good about it. I don't want to do it, and I won't. Will you accept this?" If a masculine husband is smart, he'll compromise with you rather than demand unconditional compliance. And if you're a feeling-centered, feminine-energy person, you'll hear out your masculine-energy man graciously and use as much of his solution as you can. At the same time, he accepts your right to incorporate his suggestions into your own solution. Equations that are all or nothing, black or white, create confrontations that ruin intimacy and romance.

Don't try to earn his respect. Unfortunately, the more you intimidate a masculine man with your respectability, the less he'll see you as sexually desirable. Men with masculine-based energy want to make love to women who want to be cherished, rather than women who want to be respected. Go outside the relationship for respect. Your career, job, volunteer work, hobbies, or education can be places where you can earn it. Within the marriage, you want your feelings to be cherished.

## The Equal Career Couple

Although I do believe that there are only two games in town, involving money (male) and sex (female), in this day and age, simultaneous careers of equal financial reward are common. Often, the feminine energy makes more money than the male. How do you make the relationship work? By making sure that the two people flow with the energy exchange and don't trample one another. In other words, who is respected, and who is cherished? Even if the feminine energy makes more money than the male, the issue is still who is the active, giving, masculine energy and who is the passive, receptive, feminine energy.

Jerome, an associate professor of literature, made about half as much money as his girlfriend, Suzette, a caterer. However, Jerome was clearly the male in the relationship, and Suzette admired and respected his position and intellect. As the cherished one, she brought sensuality into the life of the couple. When Jerome went to Suzette's apartment after work, he could relax. She provided a comfortable and loving environment.

After nine months of a mutually monogamous, long-term sexual relationship, Suzette knew she wanted to marry Jerome. She still tingled when he told her decisively what he wanted, whether it was a date or making love. She needed her man to be the leader in the relationship, and when Jerome led her to where he wanted her to go, she responded sensuously and sexually. She was able to do this because she felt secure, which was necessary for her to be sexually open and vulnerable.

And Jerome loved her vulnerability. It was a sexual turn-on for him to control her pleasure with his own hands. He knew she trusted him, and because she did, he could take more risks and be more creative about leading and pleasing her sexually. She brought out his masculinity sexually, and he brought out her femininity sexually. This sealed their intimacy. For Suzette and Jerome, who are now married, the relationship was balanced. His first priority was to be respected, and hers was to be cherished.

Being equal in career and brains doesn't mean being equal in energy preference. Everyone has innate talents and preferences. One person likes to make reservations or pay bills, while the other likes to cook or prefers initiating sex. When a man and woman are equal in career and brains, they can talk about likes and preferences and personal talents that make one of them better suited to perform some of the various mental and physical tasks required of a couple. Beware of men who, to keep a painful distance between you, will neither respect nor cherish you. They are afraid of intimacy. Superficiality is the goal of nonintimate people. Getting money and having sex are the goals of superficial couples. Sharing feelings and thoughts are the goals of truly loving vulnerable men and women.

## Is Giving Masculine or Feminine?

Giving is masculine energy. Feminine energy is not giving because giving is active, and femininity, whether in women or men, is passive. Feminine energy is receiving and giving back. For a balance of energy, feminine-energy women or men must give back to Masculine-energy men or women, who first graciously give, protect, and cherish them.

A masculine-energy man doesn't marry a woman who gives to him unless he's a little boy who wants to be mothered. A masculine-energy man marries a feminine-energy woman, who's available to receive from him, who respects him for giving, and who knows how to give back to reward him, but always a little less than he gives. She doesn't give back more than he has given her.

In a rational family, a woman is taught to love herself first. If, however, she is raised in a family where her feminine father wanted his feelings taken care of before his wife's or his daughter's (and didn't give back lovingly), she cannot develop self-love.

Many women have been trained by their fathers to be another mommy and taught that giving is a feminine skill while receiving is the right and privilege of the real man. An example of this kind of man is an alcoholic, a workaholic, someone who is violent or abusive, or who has high-performance expectations of his daughter. When these daughters grow up, they feel they have to get out there and do something for a man to love them. A young woman who isn't cherished by her father but is only validated by him if she performs will usually be a mother to the men in her life.

If you look back at your own childhood and remember your mother as giving, protecting, and cherishing her family, you see someone who forgot to go back to her womanhood after she had her babies. Unfortunately, many women never get over an attack of motherhood.

According to Jung, at the core of a woman resides a masculine energy called the "animus." This energy, we see, can be used as an "anchor," a "claw," or a "shovel of love."

A woman who is an anchor says no to whatever doesn't feel good to her, and requires information to help her say yes comfortably.

A claw woman uses her youth, beauty, money, power, and prestige to use and abuse the men in her life. A claw woman may have been raised by her daddy to be spoiled by men. No limits were set for her. She's selfish and takes what she wants without equity.

A claw woman drains her loved ones until they die or leave. She is a perpetual little child, not a wife or mother. A claw woman survives only as long as she maintains her assets. When they go with age, she usually ends up being a pathetic shoveller trying to get love by spoiling men.

A woman who's a shovel of love says yes to whatever her loved ones request, no matter her doubts, and invites her spoiled man and children to use and abuse her. A shovel woman is the perpetual giving mother who hopes that someday her loved ones will reward her for giving up her life. But they never do.

It's healthy to be an anchorwoman who causes pain by saying no to loved ones, especially men, because you hurt yourself by saying yes too much. Saying no helps her man learn to share love. An anchorwoman can inspire her man to be more generous, more protective, and more cherishing by requiring him to do it or lose her love.

Many masculine men test their wives by seeing if they will mother them physically. What they really need is a woman who won't love them like a giving mother, but rather as a self-centered, receiving female. Women who mother their husbands eventually either drive them away or subdue them until they cannot stand alone.

Motherhood should end when a woman's son is around ten years old. At that point, she should switch back to being self-centered. If she continues mothering her boy, he'll never become a generous, protective, cherishing man. Instead, he'll remain a *puer aeternus*, a Peter Pan, a narcissistic little boy who hasn't grown into healthy manhood. He won't have the ability to love, protect, or cherish, and he won't give back or assume responsibility. He'll marry a shovel woman and request more, better, and different services as long as she doesn't anchor herself in self-centered love. He'll demand that his wife and daughters serve him and his sons.

Only a Peter Pan-type man expects his woman to take better care of him than of herself. For this immature little boy-man, giving to a woman first is unthinkable. He wants her to give to him, as his mom gave to his dad. Mommy gives to you because mommy loves you better than herself. She would do anything for you. She has been put on earth for the sole purpose of giving
to you.

Beware. Once you start giving to a Peter Pan, he won't let you stop. He's insatiable, like a 2-year-old boy. Of course, since having sex with their mommy is a no-no, these men eventually stop having sex with their women mommies and instead take mistresses.

It's fine to give to little children and sick people but dangerous to give to able-bodied people. A codependent woman buys their love because she doesn't feel worthy of it unless she performs.

Lucille, 42, had separated from Bill, 48, over his gambling problem. She was sick of the struggle to keep their home afloat. Bill joined Gamblers Anonymous shortly after their separation, and they became lovers again. As fate would have it, he was soon laid off after fifteen years with his sales company. He asked if he might move back home since he and Lucille were getting along so well. In a session with them, I counseled that only feminine-energy men and women like to live in the space of the masculine-energy leader and protector, so that Bill's needing Lucille to help him financially could turn Lucille off. I advised him to earn her respect by solving his money problems before the two of them lived together again. I also told Lucille to commit to the marriage, not to rescue Bill like a son.

If you're a healthy, feminine-energy woman, you're self-centered. You love yourself before any man. Then you share that love with your masculine-energy man and your loved ones. You say no to people, places, and things that hurt you in any way. You say no to whatever strikes you as wrong. You say no to the man you love. You say, "I don't feel good about doing what you ask, and I will not do it, even if it causes you pain. I would rather cause you pain by saying no than hurt myself by saying yes." Sometimes you must also say, "I'm not going to put up with what you do. I'm going to leave you now."

A masculine-energy man must love his feminine-energy woman better than himself, or he'll use and abuse her if she allows it. If you can learn to say no, you'll have the satisfaction of knowing that you can never be used by a man. Remember, if it doesn't feel right, don't do it.

Leonora, 36, had been raised to spoil her man so that he would never leave her, but after twelve years, she was burned out. Her husband, Don, expected her to work outside the home, take care of their three boys, dress up twenty-four hours a day, be ready to go out with him every night and have great sex when they came home. Leonora was depressed and angry but didn't know what to do.

I could see that Leonora had been a shovel full of love for her husband for years while neglecting to set boundaries for herself. My guess is that she rarely said to him, "No, I don't want to do what you ask. It doesn't feel good to me or for me."

But Leonora had finally reached the end of her shovel, and I advised her to speak up, using my communication tools. I said, "Begin to anchor yourself by saying no respectfully. He'll be in pain and may yell and have tantrums for a while, even as long as eight weeks, because it can take that long for him to process a decision. As long as he's not violent, accept his tactics and anchor yourself in the storm. If he leaves, let him go and mark off eight weeks. Let him cool off in his bear cave."

In his book, Men Are from Mars, Women Are from Venus, John Gray speaks of the "bear cave" into which men retreat. Often, a man must go into his bear cave to stew in his feelings a while before he comes out and shares them because men segregate their left lobe verbal thinking from their right lobe nonverbal feelings. They need time, quiet, and solitude to work through their negative feelings.

You won't gain any points arguing with him. Men (especially right-handed men) can focus their logic better than women. Our best argument is respectful, passive silence while we listen. He'll hear himself when we're quiet.

I ask women who give too much to make this pledge: "I promise, on my honor, never to give anything to an able-bodied person, especially a man, over the age of ten, unless I get what I want (cherishing) first.'

## When You Say Receiver, I Hear Taker

Milt, 48, came to one of my seminars with his friend Dave, 50. Both men had been married a couple of times and felt taken by women. They were cynical and had vowed never to marry again. After listening to me talk about giving and receiving and giving back, Milt raised his hand and said, "When you say receiver, I hear taker. A voice in my mind says, 'selfish, spoiled, dumb blond bimbo.' This can't be what you're talking about. Please describe the positive qualities of the receiver."

I told him that one selfless masculine giver and one self-centered feminine receiver make a perfect loop and a fertile medium for sex and romance. Masculine-energy men like to give, protect, and cherish their feminine-energy partners, who receive and then give back to balance the energy. Giving back can be by appreciation at the moment or by later doing something nice for the giver. Again, the only stipulation is that the receiver must not give back more than she or he has been given. This would put her or him in the masculine giving position.

To be able to receive requires self-worth. Self-worth is self-love and self-centeredness. It has nothing to do with deserving, which requires effort, work, and performance, and are masculine, not feminine characteristics. If you hear "taker" when I speak of receiving as feminine in both women and men in touch with their inner feminine nature, it tells me that you were raised to be totally masculine, both inside and out. Possibly your dad raised you to be this way, or your masculine-energy role-model mother, or perhaps you had neither. Maybe it's time to develop both aspects of yourself.

# What Masculine-Energy Men Want from Feminine-Energy Women
## (and What You Have to Give Them to Get What You Want)

If, based on my system, you choose to be the feminine energy in a relationship, it means that the basic qualities you'll look for in your masculine man will be generosity, physical protectiveness, and willingness to cherish your painful feelings before his own.

Generosity is a very basic trait in a masculine-energy man. If he has money to spend, he'll do so joyously. Masculine-energy men see their money as a way to have fun, not exert control. Money is just the scorecard for the game; it's not the goal of a man's life. A masculine-energy man wants to provide money so that you'll feel safe and secure and can enjoy married life.

He'll show his love by taking care of his money-making career. He knows that if he slacks off in this area, he risks the loss of respect for himself. To maintain your respect, your masculine man will act in a disciplined manner, physically, mentally, and emotionally. If he binges on food, drink, drugs, or sex, or becomes a workaholic, or binges emotionally on rages and violence, you'll lose respect for him and inevitably won't be sexually responsive. In contrast, as a feminine-energy woman, you won't have a career and money as your first goals (if you do, you're a masculine-energy woman). You'll be relationship-oriented, and therefore, you'll need a masculine man to give you status (marriage) and security. You'll want him to pay the bills while you're having babies and while you're upgrading your career skills when the kids are little so that later, you can return to your career. That way, between the two of you, work and relationships are balanced.

A man also wants a woman to be available for him. That's why, if you're a career woman instead of a woman with a career, your time will be limited, and you won't be compatible with your masculine-energy husband. A masculine man wants you to be available to play with and to have sex with. He'll want you to be responsive to his lovemaking because he's not just a taker who's in it for his own pleasure. He wants to give you pleasure so that you'll totally surrender to him. He'll take particular joy in making you feel wonderful by bringing you to orgasm.

Just as you're looking for him to be giving, he's looking for joyous receptivity from you. Not only will he expect you to receive gifts with joy, but also the things that don't feel very good, such as how-to-do-it messages. He wants you to be receptive to his opinions, suggestions, plans, and of course, his lovemaking.

Antonio, 30, needed to know how to deal with Marcella, 31. Both were newly arrived as immigrants from northern Italy. Marcella loved America and wanted to be a liberated American woman, while Antonio wasn't antagonistic toward her liberation but was upset because she kept arguing with him over unimportant issues. She told him she felt as though he was trying to control her. Antonio needed help, and both he and Marcella came to see me for communication skills.

I told Marcella that she's arguing with Antonio because she wants to change either him or his ideas. It would be better, I said, if she could quietly manipulate him with passivity and patience. The word manipulate, like discipline, carries negative connotations; in fact, both are necessary in marriage. Hopefully, by helping him feel good, even when you think he's wrong, he'll catch on to reality and negotiate a win-win situation.

I suggested that when she doesn't want to do what he has suggested, she might say, "I'm not comfortable doing this your way. Do you have another suggestion that might feel better to me?"

I told her that if she speaks to Antonio this way, I can almost promise that he'll be happy to oblige, because it means that he's cherishing her negative feelings ahead of his own. By putting her feelings before his own, he's showing his commitment to her, thus allowing her to respect him and follow his lead.

After listening, Marcella agreed to stop arguing and start respecting Antonio.

Besides being generous and cherishing your feelings, a masculine man will want to protect you. You won't want to have complete responsibility for your own welfare. You won't want to put air in your tires, change your transmission fluid, or check out strange sounds in the night. A masculine man will want to put his body between danger and his loved ones. He won't expect or assume that you can take care of yourself. Equality between the sexes in a love affair is not the masculine way. A woman surrenders through her body, and a man surrenders when he makes a commitment. When he marries, he gives up irresponsibility and takes on the responsibility of his woman and everybody she loves, and she gives up her independence.

Does that mean that you give up your sense of self, or that you don't have any rights? No. It just means you can't remain physically, mentally, or emotionally independent. You can be what I call "undependent," which is dependent at home and independent at work.

The undependent feminine woman is dependent on a man for things that affect his role as a financial provider, such as where they live and how they handle money, as well as love, affection, time, and sex. An undependent woman doesn't need to co-design a budget. She trusts and respects her man and implements his design. If it doesn't work for her, she respectfully tells him how she feels, but she doesn't attempt to take over as if she could do it better. She defers to him for the team's sake. A masculine man calls the plays, and she helps implement them so that the team wins, even if each player has to give up some individual spontaneity and creativity.

Likewise, the "undependent" man with masculine-based energy knows he has a right to his friends, career, and hobbies and doesn't let a woman intimidate him into giving them up. An undependent feminine woman has the same rights. Balancing and compromising are necessary.

After they're married, he might stay home with the kids while she goes to a night class. Maybe she supports his playing golf on Sunday morning with the guys, while he works into the budget her visit to her family out of state. She understands that he needs to socialize with clients, and he understands that she likes to go out as well.

## Keep All Commitments

Your masculine-energy husband must keep his commitments to maintain your respect. Any sloppiness with commitments indicates that he doesn't cherish your feelings and wants his feelings cherished instead. Narcissistic people always want to be respected and cherished, so if they fail to make or keep commitments, they want their behavior to be accepted, not challenged. But a woman with such a man will soon feel uncherished and quickly lose respect for him.

Of course, at the same time, you're watching to see how your masculine-energy man handles his priorities, he's watching to see how you are handling yours. Do you look appealing? Are you taking care of yourself? What about listening to his ideas? Are you fighting him for power and respect? Do you either break commitments or fail to make them? Do you fail to appreciate what he does to please you? Do you give back love, affection, time, and sensuous sexuality? To get what you want, you must give your man what he wants unless what he wants is immoral or unethical. What about maintaining your primary role? Are you staying female, or, if you played the nontraditional role, male? Often, both people find that after the period of bliss, their natural tendencies, drives, and behaviors start reasserting themselves.

Not every woman wants to do what is necessary to be the feminine energy. It can be difficult to suppress a need to control and instead be patient and passive. But this is what it takes to be with a masculine man. If you don't want to curtail your masculine energy, there are feminine-energy men who will follow your lead. Choose your style!

Here's a pledge that I ask the masculine-energy men at my seminars to make: "I promise to cherish the women, kids, and animals in my life, even when they are irrational, irritating, and totally illogical.

Here's one for the women: "I promise to respect my chosen man and his thoughts, suggestions, ideas, and plans, even when I know I'm smarter and can do it better."

## Should I Trust My Husband's Judgment?

Dale, 40, wanted to move the family to northern California, where his widowed mother lived, and where he thought he could make a better living. But his wife, Irma Sue, was nervous. Could she trust his dash to northern California? How would the move affect the boys? She'd carefully seen to it that they got a good start in life. How would this move impact them and her marriage, which was just settling down?

When I saw Irma Sue, I asked her to decide if Dale was her cherished husband or her respected one. I reminded her that she must not compete for respect, but instead, must complement his energy with love. Dale wasn't asking her to do something immoral or unethical. He was asking her to take a risk with him and have faith that the experience would bring success, or good, loving lessons about team effort in a family.

If Irma Sue was the masculine-energy partner who kept the family stable and secure, then she shouldn't move until she felt secure. But, if she wanted to be the feminine energy, then she "needed to tell him of her concerns about moving and require that he cherish her feelings in this matter.

If he refused to cherish her feelings, she shouldn't move. He might rage and scream, but as long as he wasn't physically violent, she had to let him be till his tantrum was over.

Irma Sue decided that Dale was her respected husband, and she told him of her concerns. Dale showed that he cherished her feelings by agreeing to try out the transfer to northern California on weekends while she went back to her job part-time. Eventually, she and the boys followed him comfortably.

When your husband asks that you move, either he needs to respect you by asking what you think, or he needs to cherish you by asking you how you feel. If you tell him you feel anxious, then he needs to help you with more information or whatever else you need until you feel comfortable enough to give him back respect by moving.

# Acting Against a Husband's Wishes

Clarice had smoked when she was dating John, which he reluctantly accepted, but after they married and she got pregnant, he badgered her to stop for the sake of the baby.

Recently, she started to smoke again to keep from eating, trying to lose some weight she couldn't take off after her fourth child was born. She hid her smoking from John for a while, but her guilt drove her to confess. John was so angry that he ordered her either to quit or move out, which enraged Clarice because she refused to be controlled by a man. After four pregnancies, she wanted control back and believed she had the right to do what she wanted with her own body.

When she came to see me, I explained that if she wanted control back, she must want to be single, even though she called herself married with four children. The power to do as you want is being independent, autonomous, and single. John's requirement that Clarice not resume smoking was moral and ethical. If she respected him as her man and wanted to be married, she would give up control. If she was rebellious, then she didn't want to be married. She wanted to be in control of herself.

John's order to stop smoking or leave the home was his way of forcing her to decide if she wanted to surrender her independence or leave and be single. He wouldn't be married to and responsible for a single, narcissistic, rebellious woman.

I told Clarice that she was at a crossroads and had to decide whether she wanted to be married to a strong, respectable masculine-energy man who required her to surrender her addiction, or whether she wanted to be narcissistically single with the right to hurt herself. I suggested that she leave the family for two months and be on her own for a while, to see if she liked being in control. A therapeutic separation of two months can clear the air and allow you to decide whether you want to be a married team member.

## What a Masculine-Energy Wife Wants from Her Feminine-Energy Husband (And What She Has to Give Him to Get What She Wants)

As in all relationships that are chemically erotic, complements attract. As a masculine-energy woman, you'll complement your feminine-energy husband, and be chemically attracted to him, just as he is to you. You like his sensitive, sensuous, sexual side, and he likes your dynamic, sensuous, sexual side. Masculine-energy women have a lot of sexual energy, and feminine-energy men enjoy assertive sexual women, unlike Masculine-energy men who see sexual assertiveness as a performance demand. Feminine-energy men turn on to power in a woman.

As a masculine woman, you must say what you think and want, don't and ask your man how he feels about what's going on in your careers, shared childcare, and family life. If he withholds telling you how he feels and doesn't say no to what he doesn't want, he's weak. But most feminine men aren't weak. They need only feel good about being sensitive and be able to tell you in a forthright manner how they feel. If your man doesn't like something and tells you so, you must listen and be willing to negotiate. You mustn't intimidate him with logical arguments. By saying, "If you respected me, you would agree to what I want," you take advantage of his willingness to compromise.

At the same time, a feminine man will ask you about your wants and show his feelings about them, so that you can be a "we" and negotiate for mutual benefit. He'll avoid seducing you away from your career goals by expressing his feelings against them negatively: "If you really loved me, you wouldn't go," and so on.

As a masculine-energy woman, you're still an estrogen-based, feeling person who just happens to be a career woman rather than a woman with a career. This means you'll still feel hurt if your man shows you that he cannot be a committed adult. When you ask him to do something with you, or for you, he has to keep his word, and not go passive-aggressive with resentment, as little boy-men do. And you must keep your commitments to him.

A healthy, sensitive masculine-energy woman is generous. She'll make certain, to the best of her ability, that her man is always comfortable and not humiliated over the issue of money. I've observed that an unhealthy masculine-energy-based woman who holds the purse strings often tries to humiliate her man by flaunting her power and control.

If you control the money, your sensitive, feminine-energy man may feel uncomfortable about you paying the bill at a restaurant. He may ask that you support his manhood by allowing him discretionary funds for entertainment and gifts. That's as it should be. Each person in a relationship needs to be financially independent of the other to be an adult. Whenever one person must ask the other for money, resentments will arise and corrode the relationship. Making money and controlling money are different issues. Although as a masculine-energy woman, you may be the primary source of financial security and status within the relationship, he still may be the better comptroller because of his natural or educated skills.

As a masculine-energy-based woman, you must appreciate and cherish your feminine-energy man's gentle, sensual qualities, without resenting or losing respect for him. And he must be secure enough in himself that he respects your leadership and doesn't resent you for it or try to undermine you competitively, as a masculine-energy man might do. He enjoys the excitement of your dynamic self and doesn't feel threatened by your brightness and success in the world. He'll be turned on by your power and achievements outside the home, just as a masculine-energy man is excited by a feminine-energy woman's achievements inside the home.

Of course, if you're the major breadwinner, you'll expect him to make your life more fun and easier for you after work. He might well see to it that your home looks good and runs well, and he'll often make the social decisions and reservations that will create fun for you after work.

One sign of a secure feminine-energy man is that he'll respect your decisions about your money and career, accept your directions, and to the best of his abilities, assist you in staying healthy, having fun, and making the most of your wonderful talents and skills. He'll intuitively feel your sensitive little girl side and cherish it. He'll have integrated his feminine energy into his masculine personality and will be able to exhibit sensitivity and yield to your needs, without resentment. He'll be secure in his relationship with you. He's your support system and loves you the way you are and the way the relationship balances.

Andrea, 35, was a real mover and shaker who loved challenges and action. She was frustrated with her low-key husband, Tom, 36. Andrea wanted him to strive for more by taking self-improvement classes, learning new languages, or joining a gym, but didn't know how to make it happen.

I told Andrea, "My guess is that you've tried powerful men, single and married, and they don't work for you. You bump into them or need to shut down who you really are, and you don't feel good about it. Now it's time for you to recognize that you're the masculine-energy person in your relationship, and your husband is the feminine-energy person. You complement each other as a team, which bodes well for your marriage."

When you ask how you can get your husband to strive for more, you're showing your masculine nature. Being goal-oriented, results-oriented, or performance-oriented are admirable goals, as long as you go home to a low-key, laid-back, loving, feminine-energy man or woman.

I believe people need to reserve energy to love. If you spend all your energy achieving goals and objectives, you'll drain out all your libidinal, creative energy at the office and have little left for home. What your husband brings you is an anchor to windward, which could save your marriage by allowing intimacy energy to flow in your life.

Therefore, you don't need a codependent other you, you need a complementary feminine-energy husband, who'll balance your action with his passivity. Appreciate him or you'll leave him in a huff and regret it later, or he'll leave you, because a convenient marriage to a go-getter isn't really any fun. Trust me, other women will appreciate his gentleness and kindness. Accept him or reject him, but don't rebuild him.

Never mind what your mother, sister, and friends say about getting him to strive for more. He's fine as he is. And your alternative style will work for you, as long as you decide to be the dynamic, masculine-energy person in your marriage, and allow him to be the receptive, feminine-energy man who's willing to bring you his loving and sensual skills to make life fun for both of you. Daniel, 33, and Francine, 30, both lawyers, both attractive and driven to succeed, thought their equality meant total compatibility. Wrong! Their similarities triggered competition after the honeymoon glow had left. They finally ended up in a session with me in which I clarified the need for equity, not equality.

It took some doing to get either of them to pick a role in this new marriage. They finally agreed to a one-month experiment in which Daniel spoke from his feminine, cherishable energy while Francine spoke from her masculine, respectable energy.

The following month, they switched roles and then decided that Francine was a better leader, innovator, and initiator at home. In fact, Daniel enjoyed finding out that he didn't have to be the masculine-energy man. He liked being laid back after work.

The most prevalent problem that masculine-energy women have is embarrassment over their role as a leader in the relationship. Having an alternative lifestyle and being in the minority can push a masculine-energy woman into confusion and anger. After being in a marital or long-term relationship with a feminine-energy man, she may arbitrarily decide that it's time for him to become the money-making head of the household while she stays home. She'll quickly resent quitting her good job and her loss of status, money, and control. However, her feminine-energy man may be thrown into the masculine world and find he likes it, now that he has a wife and kids and a little stability. Feminine-energy men bloom wonderfully around a strong masculine-energy woman and often become very masculine as time goes by. The problem then is that both want to be the masculine energy, and conflict results. If, on the other hand, he doesn't like the masculine role, he may fail, or leave her to find another woman.

At my seminars, I ask the women who've chosen to be the masculine-energy partner to make this pledge: "I promise to give to, protect, and cherish the feelings of my feminine-energy man, even when he is irrational, illogical, and irritating, as long as he gives back to me, sensually and sexually."

# Three Styles of Marriage

Nobody needs a piece of paper to get married. The marriage really starts when the masculine energy gives up his or her birthright of polygamy, and the feminine risks being bonded by giving his or her body. But I believe that if you want 100 percent commitment with the physical, mental, and emotional doors shut, you must be married legally. It's your commitment to society. When a masculine man or woman commits on paper, he or she is committed. There are only three types of marriages:

1. Marriage of convenience: An exchange of money and sex, in which two people stay together for superficial goodies, usually what money can buy or a divorce would deplete.
2. A marriage of codependence: In which two insecure people live one life like Siamese twins, fearful of surgery.
3. A spiritually based, risk-taking, covenant marriage: This is between two single, autonomous, creative, spontaneous, independent, narcissistically healthy people, straight or gay, who wish to face life together, with love for themselves, and with the spiritual ability to share themselves physically, mentally, and emotionally with another.

## A Marriage of Convenience

"Why do I stay in this marriage?" asked Beth, 40, a stylishly, expensively dressed woman who approached me one night after a seminar. "I don't love or even like my husband most of the time, but I'm so afraid of change, I push the thought of leaving out of my mind."

Beth, like so many other women I see in my practice, was in a marriage of convenience. Either she liked the financial security, or she was afraid to take the risk of leaving and creating a better marriage with someone new.

A well-negotiated, up-front marriage of convenience is practical, not romantic. Money, passionate sex, power, and prestige are the cornerstones of a convenient marriage. One person usually brings money and the other brings sex. Since both people generally want the best things in life, when any of the items are depleted or destroyed through loss of career or job, illness, accidents, and so on, the marriage falters and either a divorce or an affair or avarice fills the gap.

In a marriage of convenience, the husband usually pays the bills and socializes with his wife but withholds emotional intimacy. While he's working for the family, he often has a mistress who serves him and gives him sex in exchange for money, gifts, trips, and a future that never comes.

The wife may crave more attention, affection, and emotional intimacy than her husband provides, but her need for status and financial security is so great that she remains conveniently quiet, usually till the kids are raised. Then she may hire a lawyer to fight for her half of the property in a divorce, so she can go out and get another man with more warmth and usually less money than her present husband has.

In order to stay together, two people in a marriage of convenience must either:

1. Stay out of each other's way, which diminishes the intimacy of sharing, or

2. One person must do all the sacrificing of thoughts, feelings, and actions to avoid conflict. He or she must make all the sacrifices so the other will stay.

Another type of marriage of convenience is often called the "Power Couple." Both people are independent, actualized, autonomous, equal partners. They are narcissists who follow their own dreams for their own goals. They don't believe in sacrificing any of their individual rights to think and communicate their thoughts and feelings, and express all their feelings spontaneously or act on their own behalf. They relate only if it suits their needs. When their narcissistic independence is confronted, they scream, "You are trying to control me. I have a right to be myself."

# A Codependent Marriage

It felt so good to be together all the time. Frances, 30, needed to be needed, and Leonard, 33, fulfilled her needs. They met on the slopes of a local ski run and it seemed they never parted. Early engagement and a lovely wedding followed within the first year of their knowing each other.

Leonard was eager to please and respected all of Frances's requests, but she was feeling smothered after a year and a half of this proximity. Her former codependent neediness had been fulfilled by Leonard, and now she wanted space to fly. But everything she did alone or with friends, without Leonard, caused him anguish, which in turn caused Frances guilt.

Frances was in a codependent marriage. A codependent symbiotic marriage is one in which one person absorbs the other. In a codependent marriage, the goal isn't money and sex; it's emotional, symbiotic security. It's as if a big fish swallows a little fish who agrees to be eaten alive. The big fish is a narcissistic, independent, and overly controlling person, male or female, who wants his or her thoughts and feelings put in the number one position. The little narcissistically deprived fish mate has so little self-esteem that he or she allows himself or herself to be treated as a victim, or martyr, rather than as a person. As sad as this is, even worse is how grateful the little fish is to be eaten up by the big fish narcissist, and how comfortable he or she feels as a nonperson.

The intimacy created is so codependent and absorbing that there is little space for either partner to grow. The slave needs its master and vice versa. Any cleavage results in the pain of abandonment and rejection. When one of the partners emerges from the death grip of the other, the marriage usually falls apart.

Frances had been such a person. But now things had changed. In a relationship workshop I ran at her company, she asked me what to do. I told her, "You can't teach anyone. You can only demonstrate. Even if he doesn't feel good about you doing other things in your life besides marriage, let him decide the price he will pay, which could be divorce, separation, pouting, depression, or illness.

"Accept him as is unless you're getting sick of being around a toxic person and then leave."

## A Covenant Marriage

The highest spiritual form of marriage is the covenant marriage. My analogy is that two independent companies decide to merge into a single corporation.

A covenant marriage consists of two single, healthy narcissists who decide to give up some independence and lack of responsibility to marry. Their goal for marriage is to expand and enhance their individual lives by forming a team. Their covenant is to support each other's individuality while giving up their narcissistic rights to be respected and cherished equally. It's based on freedom of choice and a willingness to give up narcissistic selfishness in exchange for respectability, money, security, and social status, as well as cherishing, sensuality, homemaking, and sexual security.

A covenant is formed by a feminine-energy person who's grounded in his or her worthiness and desirability, and by a masculine-energy person who's grounded in his or her competence and adequacy. The feminine-energy person magnetizes the masculine-energy person, who is then generous and giving to the feminine-energy person (who requires receiving before giving back).

The covenant couple negotiates a mutual interdependency and become a balanced unit in the world for the greater good of their love and spirituality, which is their goal in life. If the two people don't have a purpose for their relationship other than sexual gratification, it won't work. Only the soul, never the body, can really be satisfied.

A covenant marriage combines chemistry (physical lust), compatibility (mind liking), and the ability to communicate verbally and nonverbally what each person wants and doesn't want. The couple must communicate without resorting to intimidation through fear and abuse tactics or using a partner's lack of self-esteem to seduce him or her into submission.

In marriage, bodies commit sexually and sensually. The mind commits to money, property and status in the community.

When the body and the mind are committed, you have Like, Love, and Lust, and then and only then is the person in love. To love and be loved is the ultimate spiritual goal of all good people. I don't believe in divorce-legal or emotional, as long as there is any piece of love left. Love is so hard to come by that when you do get a little of it, you should nurture it to the very end.

## How to Relate to Your Man

There are three ways you can relate to your man:

1. You can accept him, which means that you may not always like or approve of what he is and does, but you find more assets than liabilities and you want to stay with him. To accept a man is to love him even when you don't always approve of his behavior. If you get someone who is at least 51 percent, keep that person. That is, if you like more about the person than you don't, then keep him. The odds are that if you don't, and go out looking for a better deal, you could end up with someone who's 48 percent or less. If a man's assets outweigh his liabilities, stay with him. If they don't, get out early.

2. You can reject him, which means that there are irreconcilable differences between you, that you cannot, in good conscience, get past. Does rejection mean the end of a relationship? Not necessarily. When you come across behavior that you know you cannot approve of, you can talk about it using the tools of communication in this book.

We all have qualities we could eliminate or improve, but we rarely do so when a gun is put to our head. Humans grow and bloom in loving, accepting relationships. When you see your lover doing something you hate, ask yourself whether it's bad enough to warrant your rejecting him; then either accept or reject him.

I suggest that you save total rejection for moral and ethical issues such as dishonesty or violence, or if he is a chronic cad or displays insensitive behavior. In other words, total rejection is for things which, if you stay, indicate your complicity. Little faults deserve little rejections and lots of love both ways.

3. You tolerate him, which is to half accept (love) and half reject (dislike) him. This is teeter-tottering. It promotes mood swings, which are difficult for you both. To tolerate is the only destructive thing in a romance. When you tolerate lateness, sloppiness, being overweight, burps, expelling of gas, lying, selfishness, cheating, cheapness, or insensitivity, you hurt yourself by failing your own sense of virtue and integrity.

Tolerating is a codependent game practiced by narcissistically deprived men and women. From zero on the narcissistic scale of one to ten, we must aspire to a full ten human being rather than be a one. To acquire a broken human is like going to a swap meet to buy a cheap, secondhand item rather than spending the money to get a new one because you are worth a new, unbroken one. Narcissists of either sex tolerate others' imperfections from their place of perceived perfection. To be around these people is to live under a microscope. They constantly teach, preach, criticize, and rebuild others to their standards. Of course, they fail and move on. When they meet their match, another perfect narcissist, the war is on.

So, you have only two choices: to accept him as he is, as long as he has one or two of the nonnegotiable items you require and is moral and ethical; or to reject him cleanly and kindly. Don't try to retrain him through lectures, arguments, put-downs, or criticism, which damages his image of you as a sensitive, receptive, accepting woman, and does little good. Don't try to rebuild him. When you do, you're acting like a mother, and you're using masculine energy. If you get the job done, he becomes your feminine-energy man, and you may lose respect for him, while he gains respect for you at the cost of cherishing you. Whatever you find missing in him, you can get from other sources. If he isn't crazy about ballet, go with a girlfriend or relative. If he doesn't have a jacket you like, give him one for Christmas or his birthday for you.

When people are loved and accepted, they hear what you're saying and can choose either to modify their behavior or to pay the price of rejection by you. When you criticize or hassle people, you're being righteous and judgmental and exhibiting your dark side.

Joanna, an assistant marketing manager, disliked the fact that her husband, Donald, an architect, would plan things for them to do without consulting her. I suggested she say, "Don, you really do plan fun times for us, but I'm uncomfortable when you don't ask how I feel about your plans. If you don't check with me, automatically I will say, 'No, thank you.'" Don was angry for a while, but he did modify his behavior.

Take a position and anchor yourself. This idea of accepting or rejecting rather than tolerating him and his imperfections is a big part of staying married. When you're committed and want to be married, you're like two people on a life raft in a turbulent sea. Each of you has one paddle, not two, and is rowing on one side of the raft, not both. You are dependent on each other for power and direction. Any excess power plays will cause the raft to go in circles. Balanced energy is the name of the marriage game.

I suggest you commit to the relationship and do your best on your side of the equation. This way, on the bad days, instead of looking at the person, you look rather to the survival of the relationship. Say to yourself, "I must do my part, even when my partner doesn't." Don't abort a relationship that has value. Stay until you cannot stay. You'll know when to leave because you'll feel both empathetic and apathetic toward your mate. The spark and the angry feelings will be gone.

However, if your mate isn't overall 51 percent valuable, you can't stay with him or her and remain healthy. Being in a toxic relationship may be a sign of unconditional love, but it's also a sign. that you love him or her more than yourself. That is a sign of mental illness.

Martyrs and victims always need a toxic relationship to feed their mental illness. They feel uncomfortable when they have pleasure or when there are no fights to be in. They are unable or unwilling to learn to balance the unconditional acceptance aspect of love and the conditional approval aspect of love. You need both in a relationship to be in a health-producing situation, whether it's being married, working together, nursing children, or visiting your relatives. Avoid toxic people. You can get sick and die early around them.

Here's a pledge I often ask both women and men to make: "I promise, on my honor, to accept myself and all other human beings as imperfect and acceptable that way."

## Compatibility

You and your mate must be compatible, but that doesn't mean that you and he must be clones. On the contrary, it's best if one of you has greater assets in the physical, playful area and the other in the mental, thinking area.

Compatibility involves harmonious morals and ethics, communication, and direction, all the things that make a good friendship as well as a loving, romantic relationship. Compatibility is a matter of how much you and he like each other-what you have in common, how much you enjoy the same things, and what your goals are. It's a matter of simple things, such as whether you like the way your husband dresses, the way he acts, his eating, drinking, and smoking habits, his religion, politics, ethics, financial assets, and educational background. It's a matter of even more practical things, such as whether one of you is a morning person and the other a night person.

Compatibility also has its non-negotiable and negotiable aspects. These should have been dealt with during the courting stage, before sex, because people who have sex too soon tend to think they're compatible even when they aren't. They believe that love (sex) is all they need. Often, they get married, but when the honeymoon period of three months is over, reality hits, and the two people are faced with each other's defects. It's at this point that these couples become bored.

If you haven't dealt with these issues before marriage, you'll have to resolve them now. You must see if a compromise can be reached without one of the partners having suppressed resentment. I will teach you to negotiate and compromise.

# Negotiate Your Marriage

The thought of negotiating turns some people off because they think it's too analytical, too businesslike, too unromantic, and too cold. But to me, negotiating for mutual benefit eliminates that horrible moment when you realize that the person you've married is either an intimidator or a seducer who now wants your life, body, money, or spirit. You've been taken over by a narcissistic body snatcher.

However, if you use these ideas and techniques early enough, you may avoid that moment, and perhaps even sidestep the games or the game-playing person. You may not need to waste time recovering from the pain of another failed relationship. Negotiating and communicating are skills that healthy men and women must have to be good team members in marriage or at work. After you've chosen to be the masculine or feminine energies, there are many issues to negotiate. One is where you live. Will you move into his place? Will he move into your place, or should you get a new place together? Will you live near your parents, his parents, his children? What financial goals are important? Do you want to live for today and spend, or save for tomorrow? Most feminine-energy women want the opportunity to have children, while their masculine-energy man carries the major burden of support.

Do you want children? Does he? Yes? No? How many? What religion will they be raised in? Or none? What if he already has children and an ex-wife and doesn't want any more? If you both have careers that demand a lot of time, and you both want a family, one of you has to decide to put the family first or the career first. Which of you will it be? Do you choose where you want to live based on your career or his?

Most Masculine-energy men, who want to ground their careers, prefer to live near their job. If your man wants to live in a rural area and you want to live in a big city, you'll have to live either in a rural area near a big city, or, if you can afford it, live in the city and have a weekend country house.

Unless you and your mate are a perfect match, which, by the way, never happens, you must talk about such things as space and maintenance. By private space, I mean rooms, closets, and drawers. By maintenance I mean plumbing and heating, the chores, doing the dishes, the laundry, taking care of the car. Who will wait for the telephone repairman? Who will do the shopping? Cooking? Cleaning? Many women and men make the mistake of thinking that chores are allocated by sex. There are no sex-related tasks, only physical limitations of height, weight, and dexterity.

Some men like to grocery shop, either because they enjoy doing it and like to cook, or because it gives them a way of controlling their spending. Maybe they're into coupon clipping-men love bargains. Some women have no patience for grocery shopping at all. It's a matter of negotiating the division of labor. You do it better, or it's more important to you, so you take it over.

Some men love housekeeping, and some women love carpentry. I suggest that you sit down with your man and make a list of household responsibilities, then choose how to delegate them between you equitably. Open negotiations, with no one giving in resentfully, will allow a couple to live together peacefully.

If a man thinks of his living space simply as a place where he gets gratified, where he can sit, where his woman "mothers" him, and he doesn't have to take her out on a date or bring people into the relationship, then he's going to dry her up, because she needs to feel good, she needs to get out there, and she needs to have some fun in her life. It's a masculine man's job to give that pleasure to her or risk losing her. It's a feminine woman's job to appreciate his efforts and respond joyfully.

Last, you must negotiate your sex life; how much, what type, and monogamy. You must negotiate how many times a week is comfortable for you and for him. Then you must reach an understanding and a commitment. To do this, both of you have to ask yourselves four questions: What do I want? What do you want? What don't I want? What don't you want? Then you both have to agree. By the way, when it's time to negotiate sexual issues, do it while sitting or standing upright. You don't negotiate sexual issues lying down. It's too sensitive an issue at a time of intimacy.

What I want you to do is to have an agenda (for time, space, money, and play) and go over each item with your man until you build a good contract. Then you must redo this agreement as needed. Silence, secretiveness, mind reading, expectations, and assumptions are the qualities of failure. You can't move toward a successful long-term marriage or relationship until you discuss important issues. Here's one exception. Don't tell him how many other men you've slept with or how good they were in bed. The only things from the past you need to confess are venereal or other diseases that could affect the other's well-being. In some states, you can be arrested for keeping such health secrets.

Of course, life means change, and you and he must constantly renegotiate. But by negotiating before trouble strikes, you can eliminate a lot of stress. Regularly (monthly in the first bi-monthly in the second, and at least every three months till death or divorce), talk about time, space, money, sex, and play. Renegotiate if it is necessary.

A very serious problem occurs when a nonnegotiable item is reneged on after marriage. For example, although Justin was an upwardly mobile attorney, he married Lorraine, a coat designer, thinking that even after the babies came, she would continue to work. He thought that her income would enhance the quality of their life. Although she'd committed to this course, once she had her second baby, she wanted to stay home and be a full-time mommy. This made him the sole source of support.

Another example would be a man and woman who agree before marriage that they want children, but afterward one of them keeps putting it off and then decides he or she doesn't want them after all-and, perhaps, never did.

The point is, to stay together today, a couple has to negotiate and renegotiate continuously, and that's the way it should be. Otherwise, they could start to take each other for granted, which in itself can be the kiss of death. The relationship commitment takes over where the commitment to a person ends, because a human being cannot be good enough every day to be worthy of your commitment. But the relationship can be, and it will keep two committed people together. If you didn't negotiate these items before marriage, you can still redo your marriage agreement post-maritally, either alone or with a counselor or religious guide.

# Part Two

# Staying Married

## How to Communicate with Love

To talk to your husband, you have only three lessons to learn:

1. How to ask for what you want.
2. How to say no to what you don't want without becoming emotional.
3. How to negotiate with him so you can hear what he wants and doesn't want

Everyone claims to negotiate with their partners with loving empathy and understanding, but when problems arise in communication, all negotiations and intimacy fail and give way to intimidation and seduction. While these do work, they are based on the fear, sense of guilt, and shame of the victim.

A successful marriage requires good communication skills. Poor communication pushes people apart. You can't speak narcissistically and be intimate. You must both couch your language in team love and communicate rationally rather than emotionally.

Many people ask me how a person who's involved in a relationship and therefore emotionally involved can find the strength or fortitude to implement my communication principles. My answer is "By discipline!" Spontaneity leads to chaos; that is, fun for single people with healthy narcissism but destructive to a stable relationship.

Emotions are different from feelings. A feeling flows from body sensations (your gut feelings) through the rational brain and ends. up in an appropriate action. Emotions start out as body sensations but don't go through the rational brain. Instead, they burst out in irrational behavior such as yelling, throwing, hitting, or leaving. In extreme cases, murder and mayhem result, necessitating police intervention.

Being emotional is reactive and chaotic. Being rational is proactive decision-making, choosing to speak and act in a predetermined way. Just as we all become potty trained or else we cannot go to school, so too we all must train our speech and behavior, even when we are feeling emotional. You don't need strength or fortitude to do this. You only need to choose whether you want to be the masculine energy or the feminine energy in a relationship. Once you've done this, you cut down the chaos and clear the way for smooth communications. With smooth communication, you and your husband can work through problems with less conflict, competition, and confusion of roles. Surrendering half your birthright as a narcissist is what it takes. Disciplining your speech and not acting out is the sign of a mature adult. If you aren't one, be prepared for serial marriages.

In conversations, the masculine-energy person must cherish the feminine-energy person, and the feminine-energy person must respect the masculine-energy person. Otherwise, conflict, competition, and power games result.

It is perfectly appropriate to talk left lobe, which is masculine, to left lobe at work, but outside of work, we can choose to act as the masculine-energy person or the feminine-energy person in each relationship: in some, we choose to be feminine and in others, we can choose to be masculine. Your he-man may be treated like a little boy by his doting mother; you may be looked up to and respected by your girlfriends and younger sister. We all have a variety of roles to play in each relationship.

Good verbal communication can help you avoid causing needless pain. This chapter will teach you how to bridge the chasm created by inappropriate communication techniques. You'll learn how to negotiate the male assertiveness and female responsiveness within each person instead of intimidating with excess maleness and aggression.

If you choose to be the masculine-energy and want true intimacy, you must learn to ask for what you want, or, if you choose to be the feminine-energy, learn to say no to what you don't want. In either case, listen to your partner when he says what he wants and doesn't want. I will teach you my method for ending self-destructive communication patterns in marriage.

Couples don't solve issues; they resolve them or take them one at a time and break them into chewable bites. To try to solve all at once issues such as two-career families, working together, job, career loss, sexual problems, retirement, illness, empty nest syndrome, parents, or midlife crises would be impossible. To resolve them one at a time, one day at a time, one step at a time is living on life's terms.

Communicate from your nature, as chosen by yourself. If you say, "I think and I want" (which is masculine), you probably won't be compatible with someone else who says, "I think and I want." You'll be compatible with someone who says, "I feel, and I don't want." Two masculine-energy systems continually collide, and two feminine systems never get anything accomplished.

In every verbal communication between you and your partner, there must be one respected leader and one cherished follower. The masculine-energy respected leader says what he thinks and wants and asks the cherished partner how she or he feels about what he has just said. Knowing what he thinks and wants allows a masculine-energy man to focus better. A focused, thinking, masculine-energy man will act decisively, which will elicit respect from you, his feminine-energy woman. Masculine-energy men who know what they want and ask for it won't be rejected as often as men whose ambivalence makes them appear weak and indecisive. Feminine-energy women turn off to men who don't act like respectable leaders. By knowing what they think and want, Masculine-energy men will avoid failure, rejection, and abandonment.

Even in a gay or lesbian relationship, one person must portray masculine assertive energy and the other feminine passive energy. They must discipline themselves to subordinate their secondary roles through communication.

As the masculine-energy partner tells the feminine-energy partner what he thinks and wants, the feminine-energy partner listens without interrupting, correcting, or challenging, so as not to confuse, conflict, or castrate the opposite energy. She acts attentive, regards his ideas as worthy of her time in listening, and ultimately tells him how she feels. Whether the feminine-energy partner's feelings are positive or negative, the masculine-energy partner listens, accepts, honors, and reveres these feelings, and then negotiates some form of joint behavioral change that will make her or him feel better.

The masculine-energy person says, "I want How do you feel about that?" The feminine-energy person says, "I feel What do you think?"

Asking him what he thinks allows him to solve a problem in his way, not yours. You can always reject him if he isn't satisfying you, but until you reject him, accept him and don't hurt his feelings by being blunt and tactless. Don't try to teach, criticize, or belittle him, or compete with him.

After the masculine-energy person listens to the feelings of the feminine-energy partner, he/she says, "How can I help you feel better about this?" She tells him, and he cherishes her feelings by incorporating them into his decision.

When she feels cherished, the feminine-energy person asks, "What can I do to help you get the job done?" He tells her, and she does her best to do what he asks.

The feminine-energy partner must not be afraid to say no when necessary and to veto immoral and unethical things. That's an absolute right. If you don't do it, you're not being a woman.

If you communicate this way, you'll have a flowing, loving dialogue. If you don't, you'll probably create a situation much like the one Clark brought to me. When Clark, 36, a handsome and successful restaurateur, met Michele, a stunning interior decorator, he thought she was a great match. Besides being beautiful, she was sweet, sensitive, warm, and responsive. They had a whirlwind courtship and married, but only six months later, the marriage floundered. All he could think about was leaving her. Michele argued with him on any given subject, whether she was right or wrong. She told him her ideas about everything, often putting him down, and she made endless demands on him. His career was faltering under the strain of a bad marriage. I suggested he use my Stroke and Stand communication technique by saying, "Hon, you have every right to disrespect me, argue with me, and confront me on every idea and thought I have. However, I want you to stop now and respect me when I speak. How do you feel about doing that? Is there anything I can do to help you do that?"

Suppose her answer is "I am as smart (right, equal) as you are, and I have a right to argue with you and tell you what I want." In that case, he should respond by saying, "You certainly do have that right as a single, independent, autonomous, self-sufficient woman. However, we are married, and the price for being this way is that I am withdrawing from you. I will put up with your behavior as long as I can, and then I will divorce you. How do you feel about that, and what can I do to help you feel better about respecting me as your respectable, generous, protective, cherishing husband?"

If Clark wants to be respected, he must ask Michele if she wants to be cherished, and then they can form a team. Because she has a female body with all its sensitivity, she might want to speak and act in a feminine way. This means that she would have to learn to listen to Clark's ideas, thoughts, suggestions, and opinions and respond with her feelings, not her own ideas, thoughts, suggestions, and opinions.

If Michele wants to be both respected for her thinking and cherished for her feelings, Clark won't be able to form a team with her. They'll be condemned to fight over everything till all the love, intimacy, sex, and family is gone, and all that is left will be two single, combative, competitive strangers who wonder where all the love went.

I told Clark he must teach Michele what she needs to do to keep him. If she won't learn, Clark should leave her to herself. Competition doesn't foster liking, which is the friendship between the lovers. Liking necessitates approval for the system of bartering sex for money, and approval for giving up some rights to be either respected or cherished (but not both), and to form a team. This is a waltzing team, not a disco-detached, nonintimate couple who get together for convenience.

Clark did teach Michelle what she needed to do to keep him. They stayed together and are now the happy parents of twin boys.

## Negotiate a Role Change

Earlier, you discovered that to have a successful marriage, you had to choose to be either the generous, protective, cherishing male or the receiving, respecting, available female. Now you can begin to negotiate for some changes that allow each of you to take charge of areas you feel confident in or relinquish ones you don't, with the permission of your mate. Now you're both free to express both your masculine and your feminine energies. This is the time when the switch should occur naturally and with ease. However, the same principle holds now as in the early stages of your relationship. Only one type of energy at a time is successful. If you are predominantly feminine, but choose for the moment to be masculine, your partner must complement you by switching to feminine, and vice versa. Otherwise, a collision occurs, which can undo the marriage, especially in its delicate first year.

One of the wonderful things about marriage is that both get to be masculine, and you both get to be feminine. There is a predominant leader and follower, but eventually, the follower will sometimes be the leader, and the leader will sometimes follow. In a mutual exchange, there are times when each will be cherished and respected. But this only happens when you can communicate verbally and negotiate, which to me is the highest form of love. How to do this? It isn't difficult. You need only signal your partner that you wish to switch energies.

According to Jung, every smart man is also a sensitive woman, and every sensitive woman is also a smart man.

If you are predominantly masculine-energy (the pursuer) and you wish to speak about your negative feelings, you begin by saying, "I have some negative feelings I want to share with you. Are you willing to listen?" By doing this, you switch from masculine to feminine. Your partner now becomes masculine, cherishing your feelings.

If you were the original feminine energy (the pursued), you can always share negative feelings and veto freely, but when you wish to become masculine, you can change roles by saying, "I have an idea (opinion, suggestion, want) that I'd like to share with you. Are you willing to listen?"

A narcissistic, masculine-energy woman tends to spontaneously blurt out whatever is on her mind and in her gut, without regard for the thoughts or feelings of her partner. Instead, she must signal her feminine-energy husband to change his mind set to masculine logic. You might say, "Hon, I've had a bad day, and I need to share it with you. Are you up for it?"

This gives him a sense of your respect for him and his feelings without overwhelming him with your narcissism. It also gives him the opportunity to create a safe way to hear you out. Perhaps he needs to finish a task, eat a meal, or end a business transaction on the phone. Demanding immediacy is narcissistic. To allow a person time to get ready to talk is respectful and cherishing. Self-discipline of one's mouth is the sign of a healthy human being.

Being flexible gives both of you a way to communicate your thoughts, wants, feelings, and vetoes. Learn to let the energies flow between respect and cherishing. Just remember that there are only two thrones, one for the king and one for the queen, and each throne can accommodate only one person at a time.

## Tell Him Your Real Feelings

Men who take pride in their clear-thinking, left-lobe logic can be turned off by a manipulative woman who is dishonest about her true feelings. A man can understand and handle a woman who is having a screaming fit better than he can a cool, calm woman who is telling white lies or giving false information about her feelings. Women who are virtuous and have integrity tell how they feel, moment to moment. A man can track honest feelings, and he can trust that woman because he gets a moment-to-moment weather report. So, don't hold in your negative feelings. Say no, and don't explain or defend your feelings. Men and women who are comfortable with themselves practice integrity and virtue. They openly share and discuss what they want and what they don't want and learn from their mistakes.

A man who is virtuous and has integrity takes the time to think through his priorities and goals and articulates them so that a woman can know him and hear him clearly. If he's without virtue or integrity, he allows his fears of rejection to intimidate him into lying or manipulating. If masculine men go after what they want, they'll avoid what they don't want. Of course, men who are both masculine and feminine but want to be the male in the relationship must recognize that if they don't take a decisive, leadership position, women are going to fill up that void and become leaders themselves, which will cause confusion and chaos.

If you want to be the feminine energy and your man doesn't have the courage to ask for what he wants and tell you what he thinks, but instead, asks you what you want and what you think, decline gracefully and say, "I'll tell you what I feel about what you think and want, but I'm uncomfortable leading."

He may accept that or rebel against it. If he rebels and wants you to be the masculine-energy, then you've got to make sure that he respects your leadership and isn't just asking you to stick your neck out. Beware if he says, "Honey, do you want to go to the show?" when he either does or doesn't really want to go, or, "Honey, what are we having for dinner?" instead of saying, "I want to go to the show, how do you feel about that?" or, "I want steak tonight, is that possible?"

## Feminine Women Must Know What They Don't Want Rather Than What They Want

Knowing what you want is male and logical and often overrides feelings and sensibilities. To know what you don't want requires looking at all your options and feeling your way toward them. If women avoid what they don't want, they'll get what they want. Feminine-energy women feel their way into and out of deals, conversations, and situations. If it feels right, they do it.

As a feminine-energy woman, you must rely on your feelings to tell you what's good or bad and then use your brain to act on those feelings. You'll get what you want by knowing what feels good or bad, but primarily by knowing what feels bad, and then saying no to it. If you rely only on your thinking, wanting brain, you can often be persuaded by a man's logical arguments to do things such as supporting him or accepting his infidelities. This ultimately won't feel good, and you will regret it. Saying no to what you don't want will get you what you want if your masculine-energy man loves and cherishes you. If he doesn't, he's a narcissistic man who wants it all, now. Good riddance to him.

A good way to signal your man about what you want is by telling him how you feel about it. "Hon, I would be really happy if we could... What do you think about doing/giving/ not doing it?" Another way is to ask permission to tell him or ask him for what you want. "Hon, I have a request about... Are you willing to hear me out?"

A narcissist won't take the time to listen. Neither will an inadequate man, who's so afraid you'll outclass him that he needs to put you down by not listening or by ridiculing or humiliating you in front of people. "Macho" men are dictators who order and demand adherence to their wishes because they feel insecure and in-inadequate with a secure and adequate woman. Inadequate men always chop adequate women down to their size, if the woman allows it.

If that happens, I suggest you say, "You have every right not to listen to me and to humiliate or ridicule me. However, I am very angry about this and I won't have this in my life. Are you willing to cherish me or must I leave to take care of myself?" Then, if he doesn't cherish your feelings, you must leave.

A healthy masculine-energy man enjoys assisting his feminine-energy partner, but accepts her final decision as her right, not as disrespectful rebellion. Arguing and debating painfully is not the goal. Talking, sharing, and mutual respecting are.

Bud, 50, a man's man and king of his castle, felt angry and controlled by his wife, Edith, 49, when she "whined" about her hurt feelings. He wasn't going to let any woman turn him into a wimp. Early in their ten-year marriage, he'd "straightened her out" about who was boss, but lately, Edith had been reading self-help books and going to my seminars. Her doctor had warned her about her level of stress and urged her to control it before she became ill. Her question to me was simple, but she couldn't find the answer.

She said, "Sometimes I want to share something with my husband but he doesn't want to hear it. Although I respect him, my feelings are hurt. How do I avoid a confrontation?" I told her to say, "Honey, I want to tell you something about... Do you want to hear it now or later?" Say, "You have every right not to take the time to listen to me. However, I feel rejected, and I don't want to feel rejected. I'll put up with this behavior as long as I can and then I'll take action to take care of myself.'

When you run out of patience, take action that will get his attention. For example, stop talking; stop providing services such as cooking; sleep in another room and have no sex; stay away for a few days; or make an appointment with a therapist and a divorce attorney and let him choose which one he wants.

A man often finds out how he feels about his wife and his marriage only after she's left him. During the separation, he becomes ready for her to share feelings, only to find her gone permanently.

A woman would do better if she shared her feelings first, as a way to prime his right lobe, the seat of his feelings. This will enable him to share back. If she holds in her feelings, good or bad, she'll become so angry that she'll take rash action to leave or punish him. This only shuts his feelings down further and forces him either to take logical action or to get so irrationally emotional and sometimes physically violent that all lines of communication fail.

Both of you should do your best to hear each other out before you go to sleep. The worst thing you can do is let the unspoken message go underground into the unconscious, which is like a garbage compactor stuffing the unresolved issues into a container for storage. Every time a similar issue arises, the container explodes, causing an emotional reaction that's bigger than the little issue that caused it.

Many feminine-energy women face husbands who listen to their feelings but then disagree with them. Whenever a masculine-energy, thinking man tells his partner that he "disagrees with her feelings," he is narcissistically suppressing her. He is using logic to evaluate his partner's feelings and then discounting them as inappropriate and irrelevant.

A narcissistic man or woman will attempt to harangue, argue, degrade, undermine, and criticize you out of being either respected or cherished. This is intimidation, and it's a tool for control. The narcissist alone has the right to decide what you are on any given day. Their inconsistency drives people, especially children, insane with chaos and confusion.

No one can evaluate your feelings; feelings are neither good nor bad. They are only acceptable or rejectable. They are not discountable. A feminine-energy woman married to a man who discounts her feelings must stand up for herself, using my tools of communication, and make certain her children are not emotionally abused by her narcissistic husband.

If your partner is narcissistic and spiritually unteachable, you must rattle his or her cage. Narcissists don't hear or see well until they are shaken up. Have the courage to risk losing the mess of a marriage you have in the hopes that it will come back to an intimate life. Lois, 28, a bride of four months, had gotten married using my tools of communication, but now, Stan, 30, her husband, was losing his communication skills and becoming more like his argumentative parents, especially after working long hours. He would start an argument with her, and then push at her, even following her into different rooms of their apartment to continue the discussion until she broke down in frustration and said, "I give up. You win."

When she asked me what she should do, I told her to make the following pledge: "I promise, on my honor, to never argue with a male of any age because I will lose the argument and end up screaming I hate you. You're a lousy lover. I wish I'd never married you.

I told her that Stan showed signs of being a macho narcissist intimidator who had no regard for her feelings. Lois, a sensitive woman who needed to be cherished by her husband in order to respect him, could not allow him to continue this bad communication habit. The appropriate way to handle a husband who's asking for a competitive joust is either silence or
The Stroke and Stand technique:

1. Stroke: Always make a man feel accepted. Tell him he has the right (freedom) to do or say anything he wants as long as it is moral (doesn't hurt your body) or ethical (doesn't hurt your money, property, or career). This grounds a woman and keeps her from reacting in a rebellious way. Then say, "I appreciate that you want to debate this issue."

2. Stand: Now tell him your feelings clearly so that he will hear and cherish them. Unless he's a self-centered narcissist who doesn't care about sharing, he'll listen. "However, I don't feel comfortable talking about it at this time." The stand shows your

self-love: You've told him what you don't want.

3. Contract: Now you can offer him a possible alternative in a respectful way. "Will you accept this?"

If he says no and won't take the time to listen, he's setting up a narcissistic, passive-aggressive system that will eventually split the team.

Your answer should then be, "Thanks for respecting my strength. However, I'm a woman with feelings, not one of the boys to fight with when you're cranky and tired. The price tag for harassing me into a painful argument is total silence until you feel better and don't scare me."

Then let him bang around in his cage alone, as long as he doesn't get violent and smash things or threaten you with verbal abuse or clenched fists. Be courteous and respectful and go about your business just as you would if you weren't married.

Being in a relationship with a selfish narcissist who doesn't care about your feelings is doormat training. It is not acceptable to any woman in today's enlightened society. This kind of relationship only works when one person needs the other at any cost, and you don't want that. Narcissistic men want to have their ideas approved of by their partner, whether that partner really agrees or not, and would probably taper off as her body settled into pregnancy.

In the meantime, she came to my seminar and asked what she could do to help both herself and Dale. She said she could no longer tell whether he was really doing something upsetting or whether she was being overreactive.

I told her she should say, "Hon, I want to talk with you about my PMS. Is it a good time now, or later today, or when?"

If he says, "Now," then she should say, "I understand that my chemistry is triggering some emotional behavior that upsets you. However, I would feel so comfortable if you would accept me as I am, knowing I don't want to cause you pain. I'll do my best to work on this."

Only a narcissistic oaf would say no, and if he is one, you say, "You have every right to complain about the pain I'm causing you because of my PMS. However, for my sake and the baby's sake, I may withdraw from you by sleeping in my own room, or, if I become too unhappy here, I will go with you where you can visit me until the baby is born. Will you put my feelings and the baby's ahead of yours?"

Any answer other than yes is no. Be prepared to love yourself and the baby, even if your husband throws a fit. Peter Pan men are anima-possessed little boys who want you to be their Wendy mama, even when you are pregnant or have children. Potty train his narcissism now before the baby is born, or you'll have two babies to contend with. One can hurt you physically, mentally, and emotionally, and the other counts on you because it's helpless.

## He Puts Her Down

When Malcolm, 34, felt that Barbara, 21, made him angry, he used his mouth like a stiletto, hurting her badly by insulting her intelligence and abilities and calling her ugly names.

She'd watched his mother do the same thing to his alcoholic dad, so most of the time she ignored his behavior. She loved him, and, in all other ways, he was a stable, secure man who basically acted appropriately. But because she feared these outbursts, she'd molded herself into a wife who anticipated his reactions and avoided making him angry, often at the cost of expressing her feelings. At one of my seminars, she asked me what she should do.

Feelings, I told her, can be triggered by people, places, and things, but only children and immature adults are unable to channel their feelings through their brain before speaking or doing.

Impulsive and compulsive behavior is caused by either a neurological disability, such as Attention Deficit Disorder (ADD), or some other medical or psychological problem that is beyond someone's control. Barbara's husband might have needed medical or psychological therapy to enable him to discipline his emotions.

Name-calling is used by inadequate men and women who tear down adequate people to feel more secure within themselves. If Barbara refused to put up with her husband's tirades, he would either leave to find a better codependent mommy or he would get help. Either way, she wins.

Ron, 45, always needed to be the center of attention, especially when Marilyn, 40, showed herself as a bright, verbal, and interesting woman. Whenever she told a story, especially in front of others, he would interrupt her, correct details, and generally cause her to lose confidence in herself. Marilyn came to a seminar and asked what she could do for her marriage. I said, "Your husband feels inadequate, insecure, and undesirable next to you. If you allow him to interrupt or correct you in public (or private), you have low self-esteem. You must require him to either respect you enough to keep his mouth shut until you have finished or cherish you enough not to humiliate you."

I told her that to break up his bad habit, she needed to use the Clean Up technique. She should say, "Honey, I want to talk with you about how we communicate, especially in front of people. Do you want to talk now or at a better time?"

Hopefully, he'll say, "Now is fine," or "After dinner is better." When he says okay, continue by saying, "Dear, you have every right to interrupt me when I'm speaking and even to correct me on the spot. However, when you do, I feel so unloved and uncherished and humiliated that I no longer want to risk such behavior, especially in public. If you're unwilling to treat me as your loving wife, I'll refuse to go with you. I'll refuse to continue a conversation in which you've interrupted or corrected me until you apologize and listen to what I have to say. If we're out socially and you continue to cause me to feel humiliated, I'll go home without a word. Do you want to do this or not?"

Ron then could choose to stop his behavior or risk losing his family. Any answer other than yes means "No. I'll continue to degrade and humiliate you because I feel unworthy and inadequate next to you. I'm afraid to allow you to be yourself, especially in public, because people will think you're smarter than I am, and they'll love you and ignore me. I want them to respect and love me more than they do you."

If he goes either ballistic or passive-aggressive and avoids talking, I suggest you leave overnight with the kids, telling him you'll call the next day to find out when he wants to finish the conversation.

# When He is Passive-Aggressive

Whenever Dan, 27, felt that his wife Maureen, 25, made him upset, he didn't talk or yell. Instead, he became quiet and sullen and withdrew. Maureen loved him and wanted their marriage to work, but he was driving her crazy. This was passive-aggressive behavior, and it is practiced by men and women who won't negotiate verbally out of fear of losing the debate or of being abandoned or rejected. It is a learned coping mechanism created by children who can't win against a big parent.

All children are afraid of being abandoned or rejected. The fear of loud yelling and fighting, along with their fear of being totally without control in a world of giants, teaches some children to be passive-aggressive as a way to survive. When someone lacks the power and resources (or believes he does) to challenge authority directly, the resistance often comes out indirectly and covertly. The mind thinks of ways to survive (masculine energy) and the body finds a safe way to exist (feminine energy). By being passive and nonverbal, the person feels falsely safe, like an ostrich with its head in the sand.

Passive-aggressive men and women won't keep agreements as negotiated because they feel controlled by both the agreement and it reminds them of mom (in his case) or dad (in her case) or you trying to control them. As children, they learned that talking and negotiating didn't work. Passive-aggression did. They learned that the only way they could maintain control over their life was by saying yes and then not doing what was agreed upon. The technique is used until the passive-aggressive person feels he or she is with a safe person, often beginning with a safe parental therapist, and learns better communication techniques such as those taught in this book. Each of us has a primary need to be heard by others and to be known as we are. If your husband won't take the time to hear you or know you, you must confront him lovingly before it's too late.

Gwen, 29, felt her anger rising. It was an old, familiar feeling. Her husband Phil, 32, was late again and she felt stuck waiting for him. Not only did she mind him keeping her waiting, but she also hated the person she became when he finally showed up with that little sheepish grin on his face. She became bitchy, shrewish, and unable to enjoy whatever they were planning to do.

When Gwen came to one of my seminars, she asked why her husband was always late and what she could do to get him to change his behavior. I told her, "My suggestion is that you leave after waiting for fifteen minutes to half an hour. Go alone and leave a note on the door saying so. Let reality teach him a sense of time, not your mama mouth. The only thing you can do is to refuse to act like a ranting, raving parent, and let the reality of your leaving teach him what the price for his behavior is. Being passive-aggressive late puts a partner in a position to indicate how submissive and narcissistically zero and deprived they are. The aggressor feels that keeping another person waiting is a sign of control. By controlling, they cannot be controlled; therefore, they're fine while the other isn't. Neutralize his control--don't wait."

## Don't Get Bogged Down With Guilt

Some women try to do the right thing but get bogged down in guilt. For two years, Amanda had worked to save her troubled marriage to Frank. Frank half-heartedly participated with her in counseling sessions, but nothing ever jelled. Amanda was getting ready to leave, but Frank tearfully clung to her, promising changes. She left, but she felt guilty for causing him so much pain. She asked me how best to deal with her feelings. I told her, "The reason you're ending your marriage after two years of work is probably because you care how he feels. Apparently, you want a man you can respect as a husband and also cherish as a boy. The only man who needs to be respected and cherished is a narcissist.

"My guess is that as you attempt to divorce him, he'll snap to and start performing exactly as you want him to, respectably. If by this time you've de-bonded and fallen out of love with him, you won't see his recovery as authentic, but it is. A man who has been spoiled by a mothering, narcissistically deprived woman resents her because he knows she doesn't respect his ability to handle pain and solve problems as a man.

"Now that you're planning to cause him pain by leaving him, he'll finally feel respected by you and start cleaning up his Peter Pan act. My advice is a two-month therapeutic separation so both of you can pull back and then come forward anew. Longer than eight weeks is a real separation, not a therapeutic one."

Often, it only takes staying in separate bedrooms and not cooking and washing clothes for a man to feel separate from his mom. During this time, don't have sex with him or anyone else, and hopefully, he won't either. You and he might want to seek therapy during this period to begin to renegotiate the terms of your marriage. Too often, a woman finally stands up for herself and leaves instead of waiting to see the results of taking care of herself.

Don't let his next wife benefit by your training him to be respectable. See if you can reap the rewards yourself by watching him for eight weeks after you push him away. Once you throw him out of the house or get a lawyer, the die is cast, and it's hard to turn back. If you push him into another bedroom with no sex and lots of communication for two months, you can then decide what you need to do for yourself, not against him. If you spoiled him, you need to unspoil him or you'll repeat this again.

My pledge for you is "I promise, on my honor, never to give to, protect, or cherish my able-bodied husband better than myself, for both our sakes."

## Get What You Want From Your Man Without Asking For It (You'll Get Nothing If You Do)

If you choose to be the feminine energy, you get what you want by not directly asking for it, because a direct request may feel like a demand or an order to a masculine man, even if you don't mean it that way. Masculine men will take the opportunity to please a woman, but they resist women who seem to give commands. Masculine men pride themselves on their freedom to act, choose, and control their own destinies. They enjoy giving to feminine women and making them happy as long as this is not assumed, expected, or demanded.

When, outside of a work environment, if a masculine-energy man is told what you want or think, he won't accommodate you.

Instead of behaving like a good son to his mother, he'll have a man-to-man competitive reaction, responding with what he wants. The objective of simply having fun together is defeated. When a woman pits her left lobe against his left lobe, she bumps him into his emotions. If you are an ambisexual woman, both intelligent and sensitive, who's choosing to be the female in the relationship, be sure to listen to your man's left lobe. Please require him to tell you what he thinks and wants. Don't tell him what you think and want first.

Healthy women can be masculine without playing manipulative, intimidating power games, and healthy men can be feminine without playing manipulative, seductive power games. The women can be successful and dynamic but not condescending or harsh. The men can be gentle but not weak, able to ask for what they want and need but unwilling to fight to get it. They'll walk away quietly instead. Healthy masculine women will also walk away from a fight, realizing that the man who wants to undermine, argue, compete, and conquer is afraid of her potency and not capable of dealing with a total woman.

## How to Express Your Smart Ideas to Your Masculine-Energy Husband

Get his verbal permission before questioning him and his decisions, and don't bomb him with ideas that feel disrespectful to him. Don't let him feel challenged or castrated or out of control of his own masculine energy. You say, "Honey, I have a great idea about (where to go on vacation), (how to invest your bonus), (a new image for you). Do you want to hear it now or later today?" By getting his attention, you avoid making him feel smothered, dominated, or put down, and he's more receptive to your insights. He has shifted to his right lobe, thereby complementing your brilliant left lobe.

If he's a man who cherishes your feelings, he'll incorporate your pleasure into his decisions. If he's more logical and doesn't incorporate your feelings into his decisions, you may need to decide if you can accept his choices even when they may not be efficient, effective, and economical but still are moral and ethical.

Speak your feelings but remember that your marriage is more important than your smart ideas. If you love your masculine-energy man and value your relationship with him, follow him rather than fight with him. And don't sulk. Cherishing your feelings does not mean he'll obey your requests. It means he will listen and empathize with your painful feelings over his logical, practical decisions. This may not be your way, but it's his way. Respect him so he can cherish you.

## Don't Ask Him How He Feels

Never ask a masculine-energy man how he feels. Instead, tell him your feelings openly and ask him what he thinks and wants to do about them. A question appeals to a man's logical left lobe, not his experiential, sensitive right lobe, so he must work through his thoughts about his feelings before he comes back with an answer. When you ask a masculine-energy man, "How are you feeling?" all you will get is, "Fine. Okay. Why do you ask?"

He may not be fine or okay at all, but he doesn't want to open up because that makes him feel too vulnerable. He needs time to think before he talks about or acts on his feelings, especially when building a relationship with a woman he loves. He knows that a woman will either provide a safe place for his feelings or hurt them, so generally, the man who wants to be respected will hold his cards close to his chest. When a man feels safe, he'll share his feelings voluntarily. Until then, don't ask.

Masculine-energy men have difficulty expressing feelings in words for a variety of reasons. Because they are right-handed and young, their brain focuses on thoughts leading to actions. They can't blend both thinking and feelings and still communicate. They act from either their left thinking lobe (teaching, verbalizing, problem-solving, solution-giving), or their right feeling lobe (sensuality, nonverbal communication, sexuality), but rarely from both right and left lobes at the same time. Men like this can express their feelings in actions, such as during sex, being happy, being sad, or being mad. When they act emotionally without thinking before speaking or acting, it can be very nice or very violent.

Some masculine-energy men are passive-aggressive and thus full of rage. They often hate women as a species. These men hide their loving feelings because they refuse to please a woman. If they feel vulnerable in love, they act as if they don't care. Their brains tell them that showing feelings is dangerous, so they don't.

Masculine-energy men are also culturally trained not to express their feelings as a sign of strength. These men will often show how they feel during sex, but not otherwise. When they were children, they didn't get permission from their families to show feelings. By repressing or suppressing their feelings, these men run the risk of illness.

Of course, feminine-energy men who are aware of their feelings and want to be cherished always want to talk about them and have you (the masculine-energy female) listen and help.

## Don't Just Dump Your Feelings on Him

If you choose to be the feminine-energy partner, never tell a negative feeling to your masculine-energy man unless you're willing to follow his solution, give your solution and ask his thoughts on it, or tell him you don't need his help. Of course, that often triggers a feeling of impotence in him. It's frustrating for him to hear a problem and not be allowed to solve it.

Shan, a legal secretary who believed she was about to get fired, often came home from work in a bad mood. When she saw her husband, Tony, a computer salesman, she'd tell him how awful things were at work. As soon as she began to talk, Tony would interrupt her with suggestions about how to handle the situation. Shan would then get frustrated, saying she only wanted him to listen, and then they'd have a fight.

A protective masculine-energy man automatically gives a solution to his feminine-energy woman who is in pain and expects her at least to consider it. (A feminine-energy woman who resents her masculine-energy man's giving solutions only wants to live in the problem or have him do what it takes to make her happy without her participation.) I told Shan that she should use the tool of Stroke and Stand. She should say, "Tony, I appreciate your ideas about how to handle things at work. However, what I really need to do is just dump some of my feelings. I don't need or want any solutions because I have a plan already. Do you think you can listen for fifteen minutes?" Now Tony knows what is expected of him, and he can clearly say yes or no to her request. Shan can wail away without fear of his interfering with the venting process.

If she wants his input, she must ask for it by saying, "Tony, I have some negative feelings about my work situation that I want to talk about with you and hopefully get some feedback and suggestions. Are you willing to do this now or at another time today?" By speaking in this way, Shan is clearly indicating what she wants in a respectful manner that allows Tony to control his destiny and cherish her at the same time.

Receiving as many ideas from your man as he can give allows. you to make a better decision. When a feminine-energy woman is with a man whose brain she respects, it's appropriate to glean his opinions. But it isn't appropriate to use his ideas as directives to be followed. Remember, only a narcissistic male doesn't accept your right to make your own decisions.

Right-handed, masculine-energy, thinking men are often accused of insensitivity, non-creativity, lack of spontaneity, and withholding of feelings, but the good news is that the results they come up with are not impulsive, not compulsive, and often good resolutions.

Masculine-energy men have a natural tendency to give help, protect loved ones, and cherish their feelings, as long as they feel respected and needed. Dumping your negative feelings and requiring him just to listen and not solve your problem is like chaining a guard dog during a robbery

## Women Who Talk Too Much

If you've chosen to be the feminine-energy, receptive partner in your marriage, then don't talk too much, even when you ache to fill in the empty spaces in a conversation. Your masculine-energy man will set the tone and fill the spaces according to his wants and needs. You only need to respond, relax, relinquish control, and follow. He'll be overwhelmed if you fill every moment with sound; too much data coming into his brain will cause him to shut down. You can let him lead you in conversation. Perhaps you really want to be the masculine-energy person, and if so, keep talking and let him listen and be your feminine counterpart.

## Don't Nag

Sherman, 43, was a slob. His wife, Carolyn, 47, didn't want to be his maid. She wanted Sherman to pick up after himself as she did and run his own errands. But he never seemed to do it. She was especially embarrassed when friends or family came to visit and they saw his things piled up in the middle of the room. She found herself beginning to nag at Sherman, but she knew that it would get her nowhere. She asked me how she could get him to take responsibility for his own things.

I told her, "You can't get anyone to do anything. Your husband sounds like a passive-aggressive narcissist who wants to be able to do as he pleases, with no price to pay. So my suggestion is to keep quiet, stuff your pride, and step over and around his mess. Don't save or rescue him from reality's lessons and get over your need to be in control and get approval from outsiders, who may come over and see the mess.

"Leave his junk where it is until he needs something and can't find it, or he finds what he needs and it's dirty or wrinkled, or someone comes over to visit and he feels ashamed of the mess. Within eight weeks, he'll get the message without your opening your mouth."

If you nag your masculine-energy man, his guilt may cause him to become angry and fight with you. If you say nothing, his guilt will cause him to turn on himself and fight within himself until he surrenders and cleans up the mess quietly.

Set your priorities appropriately. He may simply be doing what his dad and mom did. He may feel inadequate next to you and like to undermine you as a way to feel bigger. No matter what the reason, take your stand and fight like a lady, which means passively, not actively. Better the mess for a while than a marriage not surviving.

# Don't Turn Him Into a Wimp

The most damaging thing you can do to your masculine-energy, respected man, is to assume that you can solve his problems with his job, health, taxes, banking, family, ex-wife and kids, and so on. You have every right to be the masculine-energy partner in the relationship-generous, protective, and cherishing as long as you and he consciously recognize the roles you are taking.

Secure, feminine-energy women take care of their side of the relationship by sharing feelings and vetoing immoral and unethical requests. Passive patience is the feminine-energy way. Assertive action is the masculine-energy way. Don't jump back and forth. Stay in one place until asked to do otherwise, and then only do what feels good for you to do.

# Jealous Wife

Janet, 41, cringed when her husband Stan, 39, began joking with their pretty young waitress at the coffee shop they stopped in on the way home from a vacation. They'd had a good time and shared some intimate moments during their time alone, but now she became deeply distressed and nervous. In her mind, Janet knew that Stan's joking only meant that he enjoyed the youth, beauty, and vitality of this girl. She knew that absolutely nothing was going on, yet she still turned his socializing into a signal that he was leaving her emotionally. She was sick of her own reaction to this type of situation, so this time, instead of starting an argument, she said nothing and came to one of my seminars to find out how to deal with her feelings.

I told her that her husband sounded like a normal man who looks at pretty women. I said, "Don't talk to him about your gut feelings unless you want to take some kind of action if he doesn't stop. Instead, try affirmations to quell your own insecurity and help override the beginnings of obsessive negative thinking. Here's how you do it. As soon as he triggers you in any way by looking at a magazine, waitress, movie or TV show, slowly and gently breathe in through your nose and out through your mouth while thinking positive thoughts. This will effectively block the anxiety before it goes into a panic attack, which can become a full-blown phobia if left to itself and not resisted.

You might repeat one of these affirmations until your anxiety subsides: "He looks, but he loves me." "I am lovable and desirable no matter what he does." "Nothing bad is happening to me at this moment." "I accept my human husband as he is." "Anxiety cannot hurt me. I am in control." (If by some chance you are excessively anxious or do have panic attacks, seek a doctor's help. There are numerous medications that can take the edge off and allow you to be in control of yourself.)

When you feel jealous, do the following:

1. Tell yourself you're a normal, insecure person.

2. Take steps to investigate what it would take to achieve the assets you see in the other person.

3. Determine if you want to invest the time, energy, and effort to duplicate their assets.

4. If you aren't willing to make the effort, look inside your gift bag from nature and God and invest in it and let someone else be jealous of you.

You must love yourself and trust your feelings, whether positive or negative, and your thoughts, whether positive or negative, or you'll push them aside, say nothing, and let your husband believe you're happy, until the big bang day when everything you pushed aside blows up in his face. At that point, he'll feel ambushed and betrayed because you held in your feelings, which he needs to hear about in order to cherish you when you are irrational, illogical, and irritated.

Trust is built minute by minute until you and he have compiled a trustworthiness record. That record will instantly be wiped out when you finally tell the truth. It's difficult to regain lost trust. It can be done if you redeem yourself by telling the truth, beginning now.

Use my Amigo Talk technique daily, as it will assist you in expressing both your feelings and thoughts. Amigo talk is a powerful technique to vent and stop the toxic buildup of unproductive and detrimental emotions such as resentment and frustration. It helps avoid denial as a solution to keep the peace.

Each day, whether in person or on the telephone, the husband says to his wife, "How do you feel about it?" Then, as she answers him, he listens to her, without interrupting, judging, teaching, or giving suggestions. After the wife tells her husband her true feelings, he then asks, "What can I do to help you feel better about this?" She tells him, and he then does his best to help her feel better.

The wife then asks her husband, "What do you think about it?" While he speaks, she listens to him without interrupting, judging, teaching, or giving suggestions. When he's finished, she asks, "What can I do to assist you in achieving this?" He tells her what she can do, and then she does her best to help him. The husband and wife must also learn to deal with their second priority: his feelings and her thoughts.

One person signals to the other that a shift is taking place and then asks the other person to listen. By doing this, the communication channel switches, but with discipline, not chaos or confusion. The husband learns how to share his feelings only after saying: "I've had a bad day," or "I have some negative feelings I want to share. How do you feel about listening?" If his wife agrees to listen right then or acknowledges her willingness to listen to another, more convenient time, he has successfully signaled and gotten permission to talk. By asking for his wife's permission before dumping his feelings on her, he cherishes her feelings above his own and she then feels respected.

The wife must get permission from her husband before sharing ideas, opinions, or suggestions with him. She must ask him if he wants to hear them. When she wants to lead, the approach should be, "I have an idea, suggestion, opinion, or want. Are you willing to listen to me now or later?" By asking her husband's permission to tell him her ideas, she respects him as the leader, which helps him feel cherished by her. However, if in these negotiations her husband answered with "No, I'm not willing to listen now or later," this would be a red flag, and it would be time for her to think about leaving him.

## Mixing Business with Marriage

Working together can be a bad deal for a marriage unless each member is a healthy narcissist. Marriage requires each partner to pick an energy base, masculine or feminine because equality triggers competition. Working partnerships require equal respect of each other's masculine, do-well-to-feel-good energy, thus setting up a potential conflict.

Arnold, 28, and Marsha, 25, were equal partners in a gift shop. The shop was doing well, and they were happy together and enjoyed an excellent lifestyle. Marsha's only problem was that Arnold's style of doing business was very different from hers. He was haphazard about keeping records, which made it nearly impossible to give the proper information to their accountant.

When she came to one of my seminars, she asked me to discuss how to handle the frustrations involved in owning and operating a business with your mate. I said, "I realize that Arnold does not do business in your style, but the real question is, does he get results? In this case, he's getting negative results. You should speak up, using my tools for conflict resolution, such as the five-step cleanup. If you respectfully ask him how you can approach him, he may show you a way you can use whenever you get uncomfortable about his business tactics.

"You should say, 'Honey, I want to talk about some negative feelings I have about your business procedures. Is now or later better?'

"When the time is comfortable for him, say, 'I realize your way of doing business is different from mine and that's fine. However, in such-and-such situation, I had some ideas about how to do it differently in order to avoid the problems that came up. How do you want me to suggest my ideas without showing you any disrespect?'"

Marsha went home and talked to Arnold, using my conflict resolution technique. Just to be on the safe side, she also called her CPA and asked him to tell Arnold to keep better work records for the

IRS. The combination of Marsha talking respectfully to him and the CPA warning him about the IRS caused Arnold to change. Now the books are fine, and their marriage is even better.

To separate marriage talk from business talk, don't talk business in your marriage zone. That can lead to platonically neutralizing your sexual energy. Sexual energy needs to be complemented. Always know when you're equal partners doing business and when you're equitable partners making family love.

Business talk is equal. You're both talking from your masculine energy. "I think, want, believe, that is a good idea. What do you think, want, or believe about this? How can I help us achieve it?"

Family talk is equitable. The masculine-energy person says, "I think, want How do you feel about this?" or, "How can I help you feel better about this?"

The feminine-energy person says, "I feel about this. What do you think about this and how can I help you achieve it?"

If you mix equal business talk and equitable family talk you will experience unhealthy narcissism. If you separate the two, you will be healthy narcissists.

If you must talk business at home, set aside a room or an office in which you both are respectable "male" negotiators, not husband and wife. Or set up two kitchen chairs somewhere that can double as a business office or go outside and sit in the car and talk business.

## Husbands And Wives from Hell

Donna was near tears when she stood up at a seminar to say, "I love my husband, but he doesn't bathe every day and when he wants to make love to me, I just close up. What should I do?"

I said, "Speak respectfully to him and say, 'Hon, you have every right to live in your body any way you want. However, I have a right to do the same and my body is not comfortable next to yours, especially during sex. Are you willing to bathe at least every other day and every time you want to make love with me?'"

Any answer other than yes is no. If that's what you get, you must set a price for his lack of hygiene. Sleep in another room and don't have sex with him unless he bathes. If you don't set a price, every time you complain and won't take action, you're crying wolf. Poor hygiene is one way to say go away, so go away until he asks you back by taking a bath.

Frances, 27, told me she was in competition with Sam's pets. She said he worshiped them, treated them better than he treated her, got angry when she complained and told her she was a bad person. She came to a seminar and asked me what she should do. I said, "People are not Sam's first choice as a source of loving exchange. Giving love to vulnerable, obedient, unconditionally accepting pets in no way puts pressure on him. They can't nag at him verbally. They can't punish him for loving wrongly. In other words, he gets to be totally free to do or not do loving things." Sam wants Frances to respect his thoughts without challenge, as his pets do, and he also wants her to cherish his feelings as his pets do. If she can be one of his dogs and act nicely, he'll keep her in his kennel. If she bites the hand that feeds her, she can go to the big pound in the sky called divorce court.

I told Frances that she had a decision to make. She could accept him as he is because there are good reasons for doing so, such as her young children or her financial security. Or she could reject him by moving out of the bedroom and ending her sex object role, or asking him to move out of the house, or moving out herself unless he is willing to get help for his crippled, nonintimate narcissism. Or she could tolerate him until she gets sick unto death and then leaves feet first.

Love is contagious. You should try to do everything you can to infect him. If he's teachable, he's fixable. The only sin of love is being unteachable and unwilling to negotiate. If your husband is one of those men, you can stay until you can't stay healthy, then leave him with his pets and find a man who loves people more than animals or things."

Sara was 31 and a knockout. She was married to handsome Brad, also 31, who adored her to the envy of other women. But Sara was in love with Garth, 40, an exciting, self-centered, aloof, high-profile lawyer, whose office was right across the hall from hers. Sara felt alive and vital around Garth; in contrast, she found Brad dull and boring. She thought constantly about leaving Brad for Garth, but she was also aware that Garth was a lady-killer who had different women calling and chasing him night and day. Sara was totally confused and asked me what she should do.

Sara was an excitement addict about to ruin her marriage, in spite of knowing better. I told her that she needed a system of accountability to curb her adrenaline addiction; it could be provided by a therapist, a religious leader, or a self-help group like Sex Anonymous with a sponsor. The essence of any addiction is rationalization leading to self-deception. The mind will cunningly take a direction on its own to get a fix for the body. If you call another person before you binge on your drug of choice, in Sara's case adrenaline, that person can let you use their sober brain to help you. However, on your own, your mind will automatically rationalize the price tag of losing your loving husband.

As soon as you admit to another person that you are an adrenalized sex addict, seek help from a higher power through a sponsor, surrender your will, and follow their directions humbly, you will stop jeopardizing your marriage. It will be more difficult if you are a narcissist because you'll rationalize your ability to get away with anything until the price gets so high for the addiction that even you can see how expensive binging can be.

You can surrender your will before you lose your husband to your addiction to the adrenaline high of chasing a man for sex, or your will can be surrendered after you lose him. You know you have a problem. Will you turn yourself in for help? The choice is yours. You stand at a decisional fork in the road on your spiritual path of seeking love.

Tim, 28, wanted and needed sex twice a day. His wife, Annette, 25, was pulling away from him and was less and less willing to have sex even three times a week. Tim came to see me to ask me what he could do to get Annette to make love when he wanted to. I told Tim that making love three times a week sounds healthy, but needing sex twice a day sounds compulsive. To need someone, or something, means to me that without the person or the experience, you would be deficient and going insane or dying.

I said, "Your wife's appetite for making love is not abnormal. But at this point, she must feel like an object for your self-gratification, which is not a good feeling if she wants to be loved as a human being. Your compromise needs to be somewhere between your need for sex, and her need for making love. If three times a week is her offer, will you accept it, reject it, or tolerate it?

"If you accept it, you'll joyously make love with a happy woman. In between love sessions, you can either have sex alone by masturbating, or you can attend Sex Anonymous meetings to learn about your need for sex twice a day and how to abstain from the compulsion for sex."

Jason, 31, spied on Corinna, 30, whenever she was out of his sight. He called her at work to see if she was there, showed up at restaurants where she was either at a business dinner or with a girlfriend, and often picked up the phone extension to listen in silently on her calls. If he didn't like what he saw or heard, he went into a jealous tirade. Once he grabbed her arm hard enough to leave a black and blue mark.

Corinna was tired of Jason's jealousy. She knew she wasn't doing anything to trigger his irate, petty behavior. She came to a seminar to find out what to do about his reactions, which were getting worse, while hers were to shut down more and more. She wondered if Jason needed professional help.

I said, "Yes. Your husband needs professional help in dealing with his insecurities. He lacks self-esteem and believes you don't really know him for the creep he believes himself to be. Jealousy is a human feeling based on our singular isolation. As long as humans are detached physically after birth, they fear separation and abandonment. This results in feelings of jealousy. Jealousy can normally be handled internally by adequate, mature adults, but your husband doesn't seem to be one. Therefore, he's trying to get control over you and reassurance from you, which of course is never enough for him. Don't react; respond by setting boundaries. "Jason becomes a brat in an attempt to harass you and as a pathetic way to test your love. If you accept him as a brat, you're his unconditionally loving mommy. If you reject him as a brat, he'll have the choice of cleaning up his act by seeing a professional to assist him in loving himself, or he'll leave you and find a better mommy. Either way, you win.

"Don't support his broken side. Do support his ability to grow up into a loving, secure man with whom you can grow old."

Donna had been married for eight years. One night, her husband told her that in order to stay with her, he would need sexual variety. Her question to me was, "Does this mean he's not really in love with me?"

Having sex requires variety and polygamy because the goal of having sex is physical gratification. Making love doesn't require variety and polygamy. In fact, monogamy depends on mutual love and creates a safe space for the couple to create sexual variety based on mutual sexual fantasies. A fantasy of the month is a great way to keep the freshness and creativity in a long-term relationship. The partners create the environment, the costume, the staging, and the technique for their fantasy expression. Conservatives would put this sex play in a kinky class, but I say it's a necessity, especially for masculine men and women who need variety, challenge, and competition to excite them sexually.

The mind is the greatest sex organ for evolved men and women. Pure animal sex has its place in the quickie category, but love is best made by a monogamous couple who share the responsibility for creativity and variety over the years of consensual sex play. New sex partners are good for the first encounter as a novelty to Don and Donna Juans. After the novelty goes physically or the animal addiction begins, boredom or anxiety generates repetition, but love and liking are absent.

I told Donna, "Your husband would rather be a dilettante lover of you than the gourmet lover of you. Since he doesn't love himself and may see himself as a generous, protective, cherishing male, he must then binge on women's bodies as an underdeveloped boy wasting his spirituality and lovability on yours, if you give him gratification with little satisfaction."

I said, "Don't accept his behavior. Set a high price on it, such as 'No sex with me if you want sex with someone else,' or 'I'll leave you if you put this fantasy into operation.'

"Your husband can't love you as a woman, body, mind, and soul if he doesn't seek to love himself, not only his body but his mind. and spiritual soul. It would be convenient to have you as a wife with a family while also being allowed by you to operate as a narcissistically self-centered bachelor. A covenant marriage is one in which he sacrifices his boyhood bachelor irresponsibility, and you sacrifice your independent ways.

"I'm certain he wouldn't allow you to be another married man's variety woman on the side. Men who want their wives to participate in swinging parties don't have a spiritual covenant. Women who allow themselves to be seduced or intimidated into becoming any man's toy have lost feminine integrity and self-centered love.

"Masculine women also like convenient equal arrangements and tout them as the new age relationship. In fact, it's a reversion to man's primitive, pre-civilized, baser nature, when sex was an instinctive drive to propagate the species, and human love and civilized social behavior were nonexistent."

The audience groaned when John, 36, stood up at a seminar and asked if cherishing his new wife meant he should give her oral sex, as she requested, even though she'd admitted shortly after the wedding that she had herpes. He admitted he was afraid, but wanted to do the right thing.

I said, "Don't! Oral sex with a person who has herpes is a risk you have a right not to take. It's a moral issue, and only you can decide it. If you have any concerns about catching the virus, please speak to your doctor, and then decide how much of a risk you wish to take. Your wife can accept you, reject you, or tolerate you, which will irritate her body, but not yours."

Tracy, 33, was very pretty and also very confused. Jeffrey, 34, had been separated from her for three years and wanted them to try again. But she was more interested in seeing married men than in having a relationship with her husband. She asked me why I thought this was true.

I told her, "Married men are safe for a narcissistic woman who wants to be independent and cherished at the same time. Somewhere along the line, you voted against being part of an intimate team with a man. Your masculine polygamous freedom is obviously more important than your feminine need to be in a monogamous one-on-one relationship. Where did you learn that commitment and vulnerability were dangerous? Were you hurt by a man as a young woman? Did your mother express distrust of men because of some damage to her and have you now absorbed her fear as if it is yours?

"Man-hate, based on real or imagined fear, results in a belief that all men will emotionally abuse you and/or leave you, so instead of surrendering to one, you have two or more to fall back on. You being separated for three years without divorcing tells me you don't want to be legally free. Your interest in married men is another chastity belt protecting you from marrying again.

"I suggest you go with your husband to get counseling for your marital problems in order to divorce or reconcile and get therapy for yourself to ferret out the subconscious causes for your fear of vulnerable intimacy. The fact that you're asking questions tells me you're willing to learn new ways to relate, and that's what it takes to heal."

## How to Have Great Sex

In many cultures, marriages are arranged for financial gain, social status, or religious compatibility. There is little regard for chemistry. The belief is that the male, because of sexual appetite, will have intercourse with the female, thus guaranteeing children. Some cultures and religions will go so far as to require a medical examination to give proof of fertility before the wedding. Sexual fulfillment for the female in such marriages is never a concern. In fact, in some cultures, the female's genitals may be mutilated to limit her pleasure, which might make her susceptible to a lover better than her husband.

In the West, marriage and romance, for the most part, are self-determined and based on chemistry-sometimes to the exclusion of compatibility and communication. Chemistry, of course, means sex. There are, to be sure, marriages of convenience in the West, where one person usually brings in money and status, and the other brings in sensuous assets or social skills. There are also a lot of codependent marriages, relationships forged between two emotionally handicapped people absorbing each other for survival. And there are the ideal covenant marriages, in which two individuals come together, give up some irresponsibility and independence, and form a team.

As chemistry has a central role in any marriage, you will want your husband to see you in a sexual context to ensure his physical attraction to you. I know that you want to be loved for yourself, for your mind, heart, and soul, instead of your body, and hopefully, you are. But most men aren't sexually attracted to a woman's soul but to her physical magnetism. Men are attracted by their eyes. They see what they want, and they go after it. That's chemistry.

This doesn't mean you need to greet him naked at the door. It does mean you must take care of your body. As a feminine-energy woman, you should be healthy and well-groomed. By taking care of herself, a woman demonstrates her self-love, rather than other-love. Your body is an indication of your soul, your sanity, and your self-control. If you take care of your body, it's a sign that you're in touch with your feelings as a woman.

Pay attention to your grooming. Like it or not, you're judged, even by your husband, by the way you look. If you have a heart of gold but look like a slob, it does you little good. Think about why you're doing this. It's not healthy. Don't become a visual washout. Take time to be attractive. Create your best-looking hairdo, apply your prettiest makeup, get into your sexiest dress, and put on an inviting smile. Just as when you were dating, you want to overwhelm his senses by looking good, tasting good, smelling good, sounding good, and feeling good. Probably looking good is the most important.

Too often, I see married women hide their sensuality under unappealing clothes, without realizing that they're doing it. Baggy, masculine, or unnecessarily conservative clothes may have their utility, but rarely are they attractive to men. In fact, they signal a lack of sexuality. You want to signal to your husband, as well as to the world, that you're desirable. You may not always want to have sex with him whenever he wants, but you do want him to make the move, don't you? Seduce his eyes. Don't sabotage.

Jane, an attractive children's book writer, wife of fifteen years, and mother of two children, came on stage at one of my seminars, admitting that her husband was not as sexually interested in her as he once was. Jane was pretty, charming, clever, and interesting, and did want to be the feminine energy in her marriage. Yet, in her droopy sweats, with no makeup and a no-nonsense hairdo, I could see she just didn't make it as a seductive female. I asked her what she wore to bed, and she said it was usually a Mickey Mouse T-shirt. After the audience stopped laughing, I suggested to Jane that she seriously consider spending a few dollars to change her fashion look to present herself as a sensuous woman whenever she was with her husband, even when they were washing the dog or playing with the kids. Jane agreed to give it a try.

A week later, Jane was back at my seminar. Her hair was loose, she was wearing makeup, and instead of a sweatsuit she had on a black form-fitting turtleneck sweater and short gray skirt, with dark stockings and a pair of medium-heel pumps. She looked both well-dressed and sensuous, and the audience cheered when she reported how, the night before, she gave herself a bubble bath, brushed her hair until it shone, put on some perfume, and went to bed in her new nightgown. It wasn't expensive, she added, but it was black, low-cut, and semi-slinky, made of a material that felt like satin. Her husband was delighted, told her she was beautiful, then kissed her passionately. That night, they made the best love they'd had in years.

Although you'll want to look your best, don't be too hard on yourself. Remember that we are all human, and imperfect, so even if you're ten pounds overweight, or you hate your nose, or your hair is too straight, or too curly, or your belly, breasts, thighs, or buttocks sag, or that you're just too tired from a tough job and caring for three kids, take heart. Your being that kind of beautiful is not a requirement for your husband to love you and stay sexually attracted to you. Men know that if a woman's body is well-kept and healthy, the rest is a gift from the gods. When they're playing for keeps, men are much more attracted to a loving personality than to perfection. A beautiful woman without an amiable personality will usually drive her man away quickly. In the long run, a man wants a woman who is lovable.

So, how do you get great sex? First, by having good chemistry together. Good chemistry means sexual attraction, and to me, it's a prime ingredient in a marriage-bound relationship. It's my belief that life is too long to be with one person intimately if there is no good chemistry.

After chemistry, the most important requirement for great sex is that the partners be of opposite sexual energies. One person must be the passionate, active, masculine-energy pursuer, and the other the affectionate, receptive, feminine-energy pursued. Remember that your sex doesn't necessarily dictate your energy. Each person in a relationship has unique sexual needs, and each person must know their preferences and priorities.

The giving, initiating partner elicits surrender, receptivity, and bonding from the other. If you are the feminine-energy, you surrender through your body, so when the masculine-energy gives to you, protects and cherishes you, he's penetrating your defenses with the pleasure of the relationship.

Equality doesn't work in sex, because it burns the energy out for both. Two people with the same sexual energy are either two competitive, lustful, gratification-hungry, masculine-oriented bodies, or two passive, receptive, loving, non-erotic, feminine-oriented friends. We all can be both, but not at the same time in one bed. If you and your man are too similar in styles, you'll have problems.

Of course, choosing your primary role in sex doesn't mean that it cannot be altered. As a committed married couple, you can add variety for spice. You may go from a feminine-energy-receiving person to a masculine-energy-giving person. This is fine and can be fun, as long as you negotiate these changes nonaggressively with your spouse.

Priscilla was married to Carl, who was really very masculine and liked Priscilla's easy-going, responsive ways. He took pride in being a great lover and derived great satisfaction from melting her defenses, giving her pleasure that took her out of her mind and into her body. But one evening, without any signal from Carl, Priscilla began to give him oral sex. At first, he seemed to enjoy this, but after a few moments, he asked her to stop.

This surprised her. She could tell that one part of him, his feminine aspect, obviously liked the pleasure she was giving him, but the other part of him, his masculine aspect shied away at her aggressiveness. Priscilla did enjoy initiating sex, but not if it turned

Carl off. She asked me how aggressive she could be behind closed doors. I answered, "It depends on the boundaries you negotiate out of bed."

Priscilla needed to talk to Carl about their sex life. He, like she, had feelings and needs that had to be dealt with for him to feel comfortable in the sex act. Mind-reading is the game of narcissists. Instead of assuming and daring, I advised her to sit down with her husband, out of bed, and communicate their negotiable and non-negotiable needs.

By affording a masculine-energy man the safety to decide when and in what capacity he wants to initiate sex or to have sex initiated upon him, the feminine-energy woman avoids problems by not waiting and jumping the gun, so to speak. Going for broke without consideration of a man's need to be respected is the fastest way to sour sex.

Priscilla did want to be the feminine-energy person, and she wanted to stay happily married to Carl. So she decided to "leave her balls at the office" and be feminine at home. And that worked for them.

Does this mean that if you're a feminine-energy woman, you can't initiate sex when you're in the mood? It could mean that, yes, because becoming a couple means compromising some of your rights and freedoms as an individual for the benefit of the marriage. Most healthy men and women, however, are able to share equitably in the sexual arena if they negotiate their preferences. The challenge for romantic partners is to communicate their sexual styles compassionately and truthfully and to be sensitive to the other's feelings. I suggest that if you're a woman who wants to initiate sex with your husband, you say, "Fred, sometimes I look at you and I just want to make love immediately. Would it turn you off if I approached you like that?"

Of course, narcissistic men and women who both want their sexual desires respected and their sensitive feelings cherished cannot be negotiated with. Because they are similar, when their partner initiates his or her sexual interests, the competition begins. These men and women intimidate or seduce to get their way and, if they are ever refused, accuse their partners of hurting the relationship. Too often, sensitive, sensuous men and women who don't like to fight will shut down and ignore their own sexual needs in deference to their narcissistic partner, hoping that equitable changes will take place soon enough. They should not hold their breath. If you can speak truthfully to your partner, sex can become a time of intimacy, trust, and caring, and the pitfalls of shallow, anonymous gratification are avoided. Verbal communication lays the groundwork for free and erotic lovemaking in which two people really get to know each other.

Don't keep secrets. You are as sick as the secrets you keep from each other. Do not, however, blab secrets of a time before the two of you met. Let sleeping dogs lie. If you are too shy to talk about sex, write each other a letter. Many encounter groups have been successful in getting people to write to each other about subjects they were reluctant to talk about. Some couples like phone sex. Do it that way if it opens up inhibited areas. Be willing to talk about what you do want or what you do not, and compromise for the best results.

If you once had great sex together but it has dried up into nothing or a ritual or, worse yet, boredom, it's probably because both of you are trying to lead or follow at the same time. Couples made of two narcissistic people must alternate leader-follower sex roles and do so without confrontation or controlling behavior. Negative behavior produces negative feelings, hardly the best situation for sex and romance.

## Two Kinds of Sex Acts

There are two kinds of sex acts. One is masculine "staircase sex," and the other, feminine "wheel sex."

Having penetrating, controlling, passionate staircase intercourse is very masculine in energy. Making total love, physically, mentally, and emotionally, is affection-based wheel intercourse preferred by feminine-energy women or men.

The feminine-energy person needs sensitive, emotional support to surround the sex act. Her (or his) sexuality is like a wheel in that every part of the relationship impacts the sexual experience. Exchanges during the day, the tone of his voice during a phone conversation, whether he was late and why, the look on his face, whether he seemed bored in the restaurant or eager to run home for sex-all the things that happen between two people before getting into bed affect the way the feminine-energy woman responds to her partner sexually.

The masculine-energy sex drive, on the other hand, is directed at physical gratification. It is, for the most part, unaffected by extraneous happenings during the day. If a man basically feels respected in the relationship, little about the day gets in the way of his sex drive. It moves straight ahead, directed toward orgasm and release, sometimes literally on the staircase.

Feminine-energy women desire lovemaking, not just intercourse. They don't initiate intercourse as much as they initiate affection. And when they receive affectionate foreplay throughout the day as well as in bed, they turn on, and they give back passionate intercourse.

Wheel sex fulfills a feminine-energy woman's need to be cherished. For her, foreplay involves affection, touching, and feeling, all flowing together as part of a continuum of which intercourse is a part. When a masculine-energy man appreciates and practices the concept of wheel sex, he will not only help his partner feel cherished, but he will also get greater pleasure because he is giving greater pleasure.

"Slam bam thank you ma'am" is for masculine-energy people, whether male or female. Slow and easy is for feminine-energy people, whether female or male.

Carol, 30, was angry and sexually bored with her husband David, 32. Lately, their sex life was of the staircase variety, and frankly, she hated it. She thought that perhaps his two beers at night, along with late-night television, caused him to forget what pleased her sexually. What made matters worse was that, very infrequently, they had wonderful sex, which only showed her what could be the case if David cared. Carol came to one of my seminars and asked me what she should do.

Too many women rationalize away their discomfort with thoughts such as "It's no big deal, he's nice in other ways," or "I don't want conflict, forget it," or "He'll be hurt if I tell him." The only problem with rationalization is what starts accumulating. Each infraction, each bit of annoyance, builds on the last until you have built a tower and it begins to fall. The secret of being comfortable is keeping the energy flowing between two people through communication.

I advised Carol to sit David down and talk with him about her erotic needs. If that was awkward for her, then she could write him a letter. A woman who keeps secrets about what she likes or doesn't like in lovemaking requires her man to be a mind reader. This says to me that she wants respect and caring narcissistically.

Being an inactive recipient of another human being's generosity, protection, and cherishing is like being a baby with a good mother. For some people, asking for pleasure is too adult a gesture and not as gratifying as being the inactive recipient. My suggestion, if that is the case, is that you allow your husband the pleasure of gratifying you, which will result in your being turned on enough to give back some passion.

The way you talk to your man is of utmost importance. A masculine-energy man needs to know how wonderful it feels to you when he plays the wheel of your senses: touching, tasting, smelling, seeing, and hearing, on the way to intercourse and orgasm. This will give you greater pleasure because you will feel cherished as a human being and not an object or orifice to be used.

Criticizing a masculine-energy man's lovemaking can cause him so much inner pain he may not hear what you are saying. Often, he'll react defensively or simply run away. Masculine-energy men need to be respected in order to feel loved. He-men are not naturally horny animals who can be sexual even when their feelings are hurt. Some are gentlemen, with a balanced need to be respected as giving and protecting, and also worthy of love themselves.

Every time Bob, 29, came near his wife Beth, 25, he got sexually excited. When she cuddled or kissed him, he wanted to have sex. But sometimes, Beth didn't. She only wanted to cuddle and talk. The problem was that she didn't know how to signal her feelings to Bob without being disrespectful or causing him pain.

I told Beth that men often perceive cuddling as an invitation to be sexual-and rightly so. Presenting ourselves physically is a part of our animal nature, and men respond in an animal fashion. You must speak honestly but unthreateningly. For example, you might say, "Honey, I know you love sex with me, and I love sex with you too. But right now, I need to just hold you and talk to you. Okay?" If he's a cherishing man, he'll understand. If he is a narcissist, he'll get mad. Which is he? Whichever, you have the right of veto. Use it.

## Is It Okay to Fake an Orgasm?

Women ask me this question all the time. I say, why not? Faking an orgasm might be better than fighting with your husband about having sex, especially if his sexual appetite is bigger than yours. Try negotiating a minimum number of sexual encounters per week. If your husband wants daily sex, you can either decide to do it by enjoying it three times and faking it four, or you can declare daily sex as a moral abuse issue, and refuse sex over your negotiated minimum guarantee of one to three times a week.

For Sandy, it was Donald's need to have sex every single night that was causing her grief. She felt overwhelmed and abused and didn't know what to do. I told her that whenever a woman starts to feel that way, she must tell her husband of her feelings. Say to him: "Honey, I know how much you like making love to me, and you have a right to ask for sex any time you want. However, I am not comfortable or happy having sex every day. It doesn't feel like lovemaking, because my feelings are not being considered. I don't want to just have sex, but I do want to make love X times a week. Will you accept this guarantee, even if you would rather have more?"

"Of course, love, if you're not happy about it, how can I be?" is the answer you should hear. Any other response is tantamount to "I want my sex, and I don't care how you feel. Your wifely duty is to give me sex now, whether you like it or not. Do it." This is sexual abuse. Sexaholics have sex, but they don't make love and their women know it.

If your husband says that you and he are incompatible in this way, it's an attempt to intimidate you into thinking you'll be abandoned over sex problems. These sexaholic men also say, "Don't put out, I'll get it somewhere else." The answer to that is "You have every right to threaten me with affairs or prostitutes. However, if I sense you're being unfaithful, I won't have sex with you, and I may not stay married to you."

Your husband will attempt to intimidate you in this fashion if he is a ten on the narcissistic scale and you are a narcissistically deprived zero. Don't be a zero. He has the right to ask for sex, and you have a right to say no gracefully to what you think may be excessive.

If you're the feminine-energy person who chooses to be cherished, you need to protect your sexual feelings, not his. To do nothing when sex is not bringing you pleasure means that it will go on indefinitely. It will cause feelings of being taken for granted as well as resentment, frustration, and anger which, needless to say, are damaging to your marriage. Ask to share your feelings with your husband.

If he won't talk, it means he is too selfish. Leave him. If he listens, make certain you make "I feel" statements, not "You're wrong" accusations. Especially tell him what you don't want- that is, unloving sex, rough sex, slam-bam staircase sex, sex outside the marriage. However, make sure you speak like a polite human being, not an emotional, judgmental hysteric. A man cannot hear or learn from you when you act irrationally, even if, out of love for you, he accepts your irrationality. Remember, most Masculine-energy men will not change unless required to do so. As a feminine-energy woman, you must communicate your negative feelings. about a sexual relationship that is void of romantic love.

Of course, it's not always women who are uncomfortable with their partner's sexual needs. Clarence, at 49, was overwhelmed by his wife Jane's sex drive. Jane, who was 38, was asking for sex daily, and Clarence could not satisfy her. In desperation, Clarence came seminar and asked me what he should do. I told Clarence to negotiate a minimum.

For the person who wants less sex, having a minimum guarantee is good because it blocks the feeling of being overwhelmed by the more sexual person. To know what's expected, to know that he or she can say no without guilt, will relieve fear and a sense of inadequacy and probably allow the less sexual person the space to say yes more often.

I believe that a couple, for good sexual health, should have sex a minimum of once a week unless one of you is sick or disabled. Too long a time between sexual experiences tends to debond a woman, as her oxytocin levels drop and other men start looking attractive. For a man or woman who's rejected by a partner, it's a short step to a new lover's arms. Knowing that Clarence will have sexual intercourse with her at least one, two, or three times a week will allay Jane's fears of deprivation, abandonment, or rejection.

Three is usually accepted as a maximum guarantee per week for most feminine-energy women. For them, a guarantee of more than three times a week is too much performance and not enough process. Illness and separation will disallow sex, but knowing that both people want it tends to bridge the gap. Affection in the form of touch, talk, letters, cards, and gifts can keep the sensuality alive, along with the fantasy of future love-making. I believe that each experience is the baseline memory trigger for the next. Building a memory bank of good experiences ensures that the mind, which is the real major sex organ in men and women, will remember good sex and will go into action to get it again and again.

So don't worry about whether it's politically correct to fake an orgasm. We women spend hours faking hair color, getting plastic surgery, wearing uplift bras, and using tanning lotions. We buy clothes that hide faults and cosmetics that cover, fill in, and shadow our faces. So, what's so wrong with a dramatic display of orgasmic delight?

If you're resentful about being asked to have sex, however, it could be because you're married to someone you are legally but not sexually bonded to. Or you're turned off for some reason other than his asking for more sex, such as being drained of energy at work, being pregnant, or having a financial problem and blaming your husband for it.

If you love him and respect him, negotiate your minimum guarantee. If you feel generous and loving toward him on other occasions when he asks for sex, fake the pleasure! Your vagina won't wear out with normal sexual activity, and it's undeniable that a well-laid man is nice to be around. Don't do what feels abusive but do look at the effect refusal will have on your marriage and your husband.

For more than a year, Carole Ann, 25, had been pulling away from Dan, 48, whenever he tried to touch her affectionately or sexually. When he tried to speak to her about this, she wouldn't talk. He came to see me, thinking he might have to end their marriage of three years.

I told Dan that if his wife wouldn't touch him or talk to him, she was power-playing him into a bill-paying daddy who doesn't get his needs met in the marriage and doesn't get to negotiate them either. "Be brave," I said. "Don't let her intimidate you. Use my communication techniques to speak to her. If she won't talk, move out of the bedroom. If that doesn't work, ask her to go into therapy with you. But if she refuses to have sex, to talk honestly, or to go into therapy with you, you should leave her."

Sheila, 24, loved her husband, Bill, but she had no sex drive. When they'd met six years before, their sex life was great, but after she had their daughter four years later, she was never in the mood and didn't care about having sex. Now she asked, "How do I get back to my old whorish little self?"

I told her that some women turn off to sex after they've had a child. One reason for this could be postpartum chemical depression as a result of an imbalance in the brain's neurotransmitters, causing the body to lose responsiveness to the pleasure principle. I suggested that she see a physician; antidepressant medication might be required.

It's possible, according to Freud, that a woman has a low or no sex drive because of an unconscious fear of another pregnancy and birth. She'd had one child, and the entire episode might have been frightening for her, far worse than she imagined. She might be shutting down her sex drive because she doesn't want another baby. If she thought this might be the case with her, I advised her to talk to a therapist and work through her fear.

Another cause may be the mindset that dictates a mother must dedicate herself to her child and not to herself or her husband. Feminine moms who go back to a healthy self-centeredness don't get confused about their priorities. They give selflessly to the child for the first three to five years and then wean the child into self-reliance, especially their sons. Little boys need to learn to be respected more than cherished, if they hope to become Masculine-energy men.

Devoting your energy to your child to the exclusion of yourself and your husband diminishes you as a woman. You will become more and more masculine-energized-that is, giving, protecting, and cherishing, and will have little or nothing to give back sexually or sensually to your husband. Being too tired to make love but not being too tired to rush to your child's aid when needed is not a good sign. Your priorities need to be re-examined. Seek medical or therapeutic help if your sex life is showing indications of distress. Don't let it go on.

Vulnerability is a problem for a lot of women. Married eleven. months, Sylvia, 30, loved Craig, 33, but she resented giving up her vibrator and relying for an orgasm on Craig's lovemaking. At this point in their new marriage, she couldn't achieve an orgasm any other way. She came to a seminar and asked how she could combine her husband with her vibrator.

I said, "When it comes to giving a woman a great clitoral orgasm, no man can compete with a vibrator. But no vibrator can make love to a whole woman like a man. You must decide whether you want a vibrator or would rather love a man." There is a place for both. Making love to yourself when you're alone calls for your vibrator. Making love with your man calls for intimacy. I know you want both at the same time, but they are incompatible because a great orgasm requires performance on his part, and making intimate love is a process of touching, tasting, smelling, seeing, hearing, and sharing on both your parts.

Sex is a mind game but also a body process, with one person giving and the other giving back. Masculine-energy women who like performance, with a goal in mind, don't have the patience or vulnerability to receive pleasure from someone other than themselves. Having control over an experience makes them feel more secure. Not being in control, dependent on the mercy or goodwill of another, is often frightening. Only their way will do.

Feeling deprived of a vibrator-reliable orgasm, therefore, is nothing more than resentment at losing this control. My guess is that a woman who wants control is too insecure to bond to her husband with pleasure because he might leave and take the pleasure away. He abuses her after she's bonded to him, and she may put up with the abuse to stay near him for the pleasure. These ideas and feelings cause her to avoid making love in favor of having anonymous sex with a safe, nonhuman vibrator.

A couple would do well to explore ways of bringing pleasure to each other. All humans have their individual erogenous zones, secret spots of pleasure in sexual intercourse. Discovering these zones is an act of shared, intimate lovemaking. Having sex without this discovery process guarantees boredom, frustration, and resentment.

Marcia, 29, had another kind of sexual problem. Her husband Philip, 32, believed that orgasm for her should happen, just like that whenever they had intercourse. But as all women know, it doesn't. When she asked him to stimulate her clitoris, he told her that there was something wrong with her and that she should see a therapist. Marcia did need a therapist, but not for her orgasm problem. She needed a sex therapist for Philip's love problem. If giving, protecting, and cherishing her feelings, and in particular, her sexual feelings, is the sign of a man, then the problem was that Marcia had married a selfish, narcissistic little boy.

Penile insertion is the least stimulating way to an orgasm for a woman. Manipulation of the clitoris is the path to a great orgasm, but that takes effort by both partners. A husband's narcissistic arrogance erects a wall between him and his wife, creating two armed camps instead of a loving union.

Some women in Marcia's predicament do take responsibility and masturbate themselves to orgasm while having sex. But if you choose this road, your husband will lose the opportunity to bond with you as a sexual source of pleasure. His separatist attitude may lead to a separation if he isn't careful.

Go with him to a sex therapist as if it were your problem, so his ego will allow him to go too. If you try to teach him, he'll rebel, so don't argue. Hopefully, the therapist will help him to see his giving role, and with good results, your sex life will improve. What are good results? Your vulnerability to him, your responsiveness to his touch, and your love for him. These will show him that by giving to you, he gains as much for himself.

# Sexual Aversion in Men

Today, sexual aversion is a major problem in men, often because they've used up libidinal energy doing other things. Libido is creative energy. It can be used to make money, enjoy sports, and have sex. If your husband is too pooped to pop, you may have a workaholic on your hands. Make certain you aren't the promoter of a lifestyle that forces him to compete and scramble endlessly for the money to please you. Good men want to be generous, protective, and cherishing, but sometimes the family around them asks for too much, and the woman loses sexually.

Never demand that your masculine-energy husband provide better or more love, time, affection, or sex. You can ask for all the things you want-such as diamonds, houses, and cars, because a masculine-energy man likes giving things as long as they are within his means. But as for intimacy, you must wait patiently for the best offer to respond to with yes or no. If you become impatient and demand these gifts, you're taking the goodness from him rather than allowing it to flow out of him generously. You're asking your man to become feminine or to be your little boy, and he'll undoubtedly resent it.

Your demands may lead to a fight, but if they don't, it could be that he has chosen to take the passive-aggressive route instead. He'll say yes to your request and then give you less than you would have gotten had you said nothing. Or it may be that he has been effectively castrated by you, hardly desirable. Women don't have nagging rights, only the right to accept, negotiate for a change, or leave.

A masculine-energy man feels safer in matters of sex with a processing woman than with a performing woman who demands love, affection, time, or sex as payment for her participation in his life. A processing woman will receive intimacy according to a man's generosity and will only express displeasure when she's in pain. She'll negotiate; she won't intimidate.

In a marriage, each partner must get and give enough to survive in it. You can never get all you want, but enough may be enough to stay. If it gets to the point when there isn't enough, that's the time to speak up, honestly and nonconfrontationally.

Understand, however, that in your position, you must be willing to leave the marriage in order to save it because if you can't walk away from a bum deal, you'll be neglected or abused more each year.

Start with: "Honey, I want to talk about our relationship. Is now or later better?" When the time comes, say, "I really appreciate everything you've given me in the way of love, affection, time together, and sex. However, it hasn't been enough and I feel deprived. I know you've given everything you wanted to give because I can't believe you've held back for no reason, but I'm going to have to search for a more compatible man. Will you accept this even if you don't approve?" He'll answer in one of three ways:

1. "You're right. I've given you my best, so I do accept you looking for someone else who can give you more, better, or different love."

2. "Wait. I've been stingy because I was afraid of letting you know how much I care. I acted that way to see if you would put up with it. If you loved me stingily, I knew I could control you like my mother. Now that I know you won't put up with my stinginess, I'll freely give you more in order to keep you."

3. "I don't accept your leaving. I'll become intimidating, even if I have to be violent or, at the least, verbally abusive. I'll make you stay, and if you do, I'll give you less love, affection, time, and sex as punishment for your threatening to leave."

With any of these responses, you can decide your course of action, whether to stay or to go. I always tell feminine-energy women to have this conversation early enough so that staying is a real option. If you wait too long, the die may be cast, and you can't stay. If you had signaled at least eight weeks earlier-which is how long these things take to resolve themselves if they are going to be resolved at all-you might still have had an open mind and, more important, an open heart.

Remember: require love but never demand it.

# Avoiding Intimacy

Talking and touching are the ways men and women achieve pleasure or create pain. Sex is the strongest libidinal drive; it has the greatest capacity to draw people close or to destroy them. Everyone says they want intimacy, but the truth is that some people allow it and others don't. To many people, intimacy equals vulnerability, and vulnerability equals pain or maybe even destruction. Adults who avoid intimacy were most often children who, when under the age of five, had parents, grandparents, or guardians whose actions made love seem dangerous.

If you are married to a *lovephobe* who uses infidelity, hobbies, or the absence of sex as a means to block vulnerable love, you and he will require therapy. If he's unwilling to seek help, then you must free yourself from him, as you'll sicken and die in the absence of love.

Some narcissistic, selfish men rebel at giving pleasure after the wedding. Before, it was his idea, for his pleasure. After, he thinks it's for the woman. So, his recourse is to become passive-aggressive, stingy, or demanding, and in general, he becomes a lousy partner in the marriage.

Michael, 35, married for three years to Sybil, 28, had become a self-indulgent, spoiled brat. He'd acted like a masculine-energy man when he courted her; he was sexual and fun-loving, and they went out almost every night. Who wouldn't want to marry him? But after the wedding, Michael changed. He stopped taking Sybil out, stopped doing fun things, and became uninterested in sex. The rare times they did have sex, it was Sybil who initiated it, she never experienced an orgasm, and Michael usually wanted her to give him oral sex. From time to time, Sybil got the courage to speak up and tell Michael how she felt about his treatment of her and her desire for orgasm too. But Michael's response was to say he was doing the best he could; he couldn't wine and dine her all the time, and there was more to lovemaking than her having an orgasm.

Sybil loved Michael, but it was becoming clear that he was turning her into a giving, protecting, cherishing mother figure who created a home for him to enjoy but who had no right herself to be loved, cherished, or protected. She came to one of my seminars and asked for help. As I saw it, Sybil was a narcissistically zero woman married to a passive-aggressive, narcissistically ten man who thought only of himself. Michael wanted Sybil to please him through oral sex and resented his having to please her. Nonintimate love was his game, and he was annoyed by Sybil's feelings of deprivation because they put pressure on him to be empathetic and compassionate. He felt that he was being controlled and that Sybil was acting like his mother.

I told Sybil that she must stop all sexual services to Michael immediately and begin to respect Michael's right to take care of his own needs. She had to think of herself as single, and wine and dine herself, or go out with her girlfriends or family. When she went out, she should tell Michael where she was going and with whom and wish him a nice evening alone. If he asked to join her, she could say yes or decline or make a date with him for another time.

As long as Sybil chased Michael, he had control over her feelings and fears of rejection and abandonment. As soon as she demonstrated she didn't need him for her recreation, he would lose control and respond like a courting male. If Sybil initiated sex, which is masculine, and didn't just affectionately present herself, which is feminine, Michael felt secure enough to punish her for not doing it enough, not doing it right, or not doing it his way. As the feminine energy, Sybil had to continue to be affectionate and seductive by maintaining herself, by being attractive, and by not demanding. As the masculine energy, Michael would have to approach her for sex, which would make her feel good and make him feel good as well.

A lie can only hurt if we believe it. Sybil believed the lie that she must take responsibility for Michael's happiness. All he needed to do was say, "You did it wrong" or "You ask too much of me," and Sybil got upset and ran after him with her goodies. Instead, she had to let him get hungry for her company and her body and then renegotiate the terms of their marriage, so she felt cherished and he felt respected.

# Where's the Fire?

Lots of people ask me what happened to the passion they used to have with their husband or wife. I tell them that relationships based on passion are often addictions that burn out with time. Passion often begins a sexual relationship, but affection carries on for long-term marriages. Hot sex can periodically be reignited by creative affectionate partners. A new scene, a new way, a new kind can bring out the old passion. For many people, the basis of friendship is boring. They want the courtship to go on forever. But that's not how it works in the day-to-day building of married life.

Courtship is the chemistry phase of a relationship, during which memories of passion are collected to be recalled later while doing the dishes or mowing the lawn. These memories are the mental basis for creative sexuality. A long-term marriage based on compatible friendship with good communication can revive the old courtship days when needed. But the truth is, a passionate relationship burns out as the friendly familiarity takes over.

Serial romances and marriages are for people who don't really want a working covenant marriage. They want a convenient relationship that doesn't take a lot of work but has a lot of fun. Of course, a poor sex life, among other defects, can make your masculine-energy man less than 51 percent valuable as a husband. If a great sex life is a nonnegotiable item for you, and you've sought professional help to remedy the problem, you'll probably either leave your husband or get a lover. But if you accept his defects as he does yours, a less-than-thrilling sex life need not mean the end of a basically good marriage. No one is worth marrying, if you think about it, since we are all defective. So if you want to be married, find the best all-around deal and do it.

Of course, there are many ways to fan the flames of sexual desire, and I suggest you explore as many as possible. Working women sometimes remain for a while in their left-lobe work mode at the end of the day. They need time to quiet down and return to their pleasure-seeking bodies. Therefore, if you want to turn yourself into a feminine-energy partner at home for your man, be sure to take at least an hour a day to do some activity that feels good and is fun for you, such as dancing, listening to music, communing with nature, taking a bubble bath, eating a wonderful meal, having a massage-anything that allows you to practice the feminine principle of relatedness.

For a masculine-energy man, a shower, nap, jacuzzi, swim, or music will help melt down the day's tensions, if he wants to be melted down. If he doesn't, take care of yourself. Don't let him bait you into a tension-releasing fight. His energies will be better spent working out at the gym or running around the block or riding his bike.

The following is a pledge I ask feminine-energy women to make: "I promise to waste at least one hour each day tasting, touching, seeing, smelling, and hearing, with no performance in mind, to preserve my feminine ability to be feeling-centered and relationship-oriented."

Sometimes couples need some space, because too much togetherness dulls the chemical edge, especially if they work together or spend all their free time together. Being together constantly disallows the fun of missing each other, which can be chemically stimulating for a couple.

The chase is in the mind, not the body. Sex is a mind game that the body fulfills in action. If a masculine-energy man never has to chase a feminine-energy woman because she is predictable and always available, like a mother, and she, in return, never gets to feel the passion of the chase because there exists no space between them for individuality, they doom their sex to little more than the release of passionless energy.

Interdependent, healthy covenant couples always have their own lives, and they bring home the exciting, interesting stories of that life to their partner. This feeds their partner's mind, which as I've said, is the major sex organ in both men and women. When one or both people live in the shadow of the other, sex becomes more like masturbation than making love. But the push-pull energy of two separate lives will cause the man to chase the woman and cause the woman to appreciate being caught. If more married couples behaved like a couple having an affair, there would be fewer affairs.

Lois, 36, loved being married to Ben, 40. He was kind and generous and their sex life was fulfilling, but lately, he'd been trying to cajole her into letting him give her oral sex. He did do it once, and she loved it, but right afterward, she felt guilty. It went against everything she was taught in church. Also, she was frightened of having to return the favor. She'd never put her mouth on a man's penis, and the idea of it disturbed her. What if she didn't do it right? What if she gagged? On the other hand, Ben really seemed to need this change in their sexual routine. She didn't want him to be bored, but what was she going to do with the voice in her head that told her that oral sex was wrong?

I told her, "Men are not created by God or nature to be monogamous or monotonous. They like variety in women or variety in technique, such as oral sex. You, as a sensitive woman, may not like new or different experiences, and you have a right to say no to any sexual experiment that repulses you for any reason. However, you may want to take the risk with your loving husband and see if you develop a taste for a new style of sexual play.

You might want to try oral sex on your husband and see if your body likes it even if your head is nervous about it. Churches teach conservative sexuality to protect you, but sometimes the results are inhibitions of creativity. You are a big girl now and can choose for yourself what you want to experience sexually for whatever reason, such as giving or receiving oral pleasure with a nice, giving, protective, cherishing husband.

Here are some other things a woman can do to get creative in her sexual fantasies:

- Surprise him with a picnic at work or a call for a rendezvous at a motel after work.

- Write down your fantasies about sex play and exchange these fantasies with your husband. Carry on a correspondence about how you feel about each other's desires.

- Rent a limousine for a few hours and make love in it.

- Exchange apartments with another couple for an evening.

- Create delicious anxiety by going out on a limb and doing something outrageous like meeting your husband for dinner with nothing on under your coat, and make sure he knows it. The mind delights in naughtiness, and there is no harm in it.

- Read a romance novel together or watch a steamy video.

- Stop acting like adults. Be childlike and play. Use candles for a romantic atmosphere, burn incense, bathe together, swim nude, listen to music, give each other massages, try naked sunbathing at a nudist beach, with sunblock, of course.

- Keep a dream book in which you write down small, medium, and large adventures you might do together. Small is a few hours, medium is an overnight or a weekend, and large is a vacation of a week or more. Look into each other's dream books for ideas on how to keep excitement in your marriage. Use your playful side to live joyously.

- Try some kinky sex. Kinky sex is like going to the theater. Some plays are comedy, some drama, some adventure. Stay away from tragedy, or violence, anything non-consensual. But short of that, kinks can enhance the basic sex act.

The mind is the source of sex, pleasure and pain. The body is simple and direct in its needs. The mind is so complex that it calls for variety and creativity, even kinkiness. Be brave enough to be open to exploring any non-dangerous scenario you and your husband can imagine. Begin a fantasy-of-the-month club between yourselves, and stage some fun experiences that don't harm or humiliate. Dress for your roles, create the proper setting, and then play. Great guys deserve great fun with sexy ladies like you.

## Rediscovering the Art of Making Love

Sex is the bonding element in a relationship. Your last sexual experience forms the basis of pleasure for your next. When sexual memories are good, the scene is set for better or more. When negative memories are formed, sexual aversion or stalemate follows, and the couple falls out of love.

Robin, an attractive cosmetologist, spoke to me after a seminar about her husband, John, a handsome construction worker with whom she was building a solid, loving relationship. Their only problem, she said, was their sex life, which had inexplicably taken a turn for the worse. John was working long, hard hours on a housing project, and when he came home in the evenings, he would make perfunctory love to her, totally unlike the great sex they'd always had. When Robin tried to bring up her sexual dissatisfaction, John countered with, "Look, Robin, I'm working like a crazy man. I'm tired. I'm stressed out. I've got problems with this job. What do you expect? I'm exhausted!"

Robin asked what to do, and I suggested the following technique. I have found that it helps couples rediscover the art of making love.

## Sensate-Focusing Exercises

1. Set aside at least two hours when no interruptions occur, either at home or at a hotel, in a bathtub or hot tub or jacuzzi that can hold two people.

2. Lock doors; disconnect phones and beepers.

3. Don't talk at all during these two hours. Only body language is allowed. Talk is a left-lobe, intellectual activity. Making love is a right-lobe, nonverbal activity.

4. The masculine-energy person will bring:

    a. Candles and incense
    b. A source of sensuous music without vocals
    c. Finger foods for each to feed the other
    d. Writing paper and pen or pencils
    e. Powder or oil

Turn off all electric lights; use only the candles. Turn on the music; light the incense. Feed each other with your hands. Wash each other; dry each other. Massage each other with oil or powder. Have sex or don't, depending on male desire and female availability. Do not talk from the beginning of the encounter to the end. Signal pleasure and discomfort physically, but not verbally. Sleep or rest.

Now write letters to each other about this experience. Exchange letters, and write a response back. Exchange responses. Then talk.

These sensate focusing exercises are designed to help bodies re- bond chemically. Bodies forget each other and debond if neglected.

This applies in particular to workaholics and distracted men and women. The exercises will enhance your pleasure or intensify your painful fear of intimacy. If this fear cannot be alleviated in a few bathing sessions, seek help from a sex therapist. Make certain the sex therapist is certified.

Robin told John about this exercise, and although at first he laughed nervously at the idea of contrived sex, he finally gave in. After one romantic evening in which Robin asked him to bring the candles, munchies, music, and massage oil, and they kept silent in the bath together, he never balked again.

John liked the relaxation his tired body found in the hot bath, and he found he liked not having to talk. Robin liked the slow washing, drying, and massaging. Together they found a new way to make love that fulfilled both their needs, and in fact, after the first time, John became the initiator of these special times, and their sex life resumed full blast.

These exercises may seem clumsy, contrived, or artificial when you first try them. But then you begin to feel the pleasure.

## How to Deal with Money

Money and sex are the major games on the planet. How you handle money is often how you relate intimately. Money problems always impact on sex, and sex problems impact on financial issues. To be able to handle money requires an awareness of the meaning of money control in a relationship. Money is an issue you and your man have to get to before you marry, not after, because money, like sex, is a potential power-play area. You must have a system agreed upon by both of you, or everything will fall apart, either in power games or secret manipulations. If you haven't dealt with these issues prior to your marriage, I would suggest that you do so as soon as possible.

Total openness is the best policy. This means you'll have a free exchange concerning the assets and liabilities of both of you. Even though you may feel uncomfortable with the subject or reluctant because you're afraid he'll think you are nosy, you must talk about these issues.

You need to know if he has ever been in bankruptcy proceedings, and what his credit is like, because along with marriage comes the joint sharing of liabilities. As partners in marriage, you're partners in business, and it must be clear what each of you is bringing to the table.

Your masculine-energy man will usually open these issues for discussion by asking you about your debts, rent, car payments, and so on. He may even offer to pay them off before marriage, or soon after you marry, in order not to tarnish his credit. But you can open the discussion by revealing your own financial situation and asking for his suggestions about the best way to handle things to secure the best future for you as a couple.

If he doesn't want to talk, you may suspect that something is amiss. Of course, during the courtship stage, you might have gotten some clues about his credit if, when he took you out to dinner and paid the bill, his credit card was quietly brought back to your table, as he mumbled, "My secretary didn't send the check out on time."

But that was then, and this is now. Now you need to say, "Honey, may I ask you a question about your ideas on how we should handle money now that we're married?"

If he responds with a flat no with no opening for future talk, he's blocking the discussion, which means trouble deeper than money. It means he doesn't want to negotiate this issue.

Asking "What's your reason for not wanting to talk sometime about money?" may get him to tell you any number of things. He may be embarrassed about his credit (you need to know this), or he may be secretive and doesn't intend to negotiate his money, or he just may not want to deal with it, but whatever the reason, talking and negotiating now will bring success later. Silence, secretiveness, mind reading, expectations, and assumptions are the qualities of failure. You can't consider yourself in a marriage that can succeed until you discuss the issues that are important to you. Hopefully, by now you know each other well enough to have built a sense of trustworthiness, which would allow full disclosure. If the trustworthiness isn't there, then that's the first problem you have to deal with.

If you're the one keeping your assets a secret, it means either that you're afraid that if he knows about your money, try to get at it and you're not sure you'll be able to say no, or that you want to stay independent financially, so you'll keep financial secrets, because you're afraid the relationship may not work out. A woman must decide how much of a risk she's willing to take and then have faith in herself that if things go sour, she'll handle it. Secrets, especially financial ones, invite narcissism and lack of commitment.

One of the important issues that must be discussed is how to deal with the equity that either or both of you bring to the relationship. If he has a lot of money and you don't, does that mean he should use that money to support you? What if you have the money, either through an inheritance or because you're a successful professional woman who has been on her own before meeting this wonderful new man? You may have a substantial investment portfolio, or real estate, art, cars, and furniture. Does that mean that you pay for the trip to Paris, which you can afford and he can't? Or that you throw your money and assets into a joint account?

Well, you can if you want to, but I've found that often a man or woman who has worked hard to achieve personal financial security or who has had their assets subdivided in a previous relationship, may require a pre- or postnuptial agreement in order to relax about the issue of what will happen to their personal assets. I believe a contract or prenuptial agreement is appropriate for peace of mind for either a man or a woman who's putting in more money than the other. Such a contract can be positive if both parties understand that it's for security, not stinginess.

The main purpose of a prenuptial agreement is to outline financial distribution in case of a divorce. Just as we get health, accident, earthquake, flood, fire, and life insurance that we hope we'll never use, so also can we get divorce insurance, which is called a prenuptial agreement. The problem is that when the agreement is seen as a battleground, it forecasts danger for the relationship.

If your man requests a prenuptial agreement, my advice is to let him have it. Requiring a previously married or committed man to be vulnerable again is such a huge risk that he may not marry you unless you can agree.

When Clark, 52, and Cindy, 36, became engaged, on his lawyer's advice, Clark asked Cindy to sign a prenuptial agreement. Clark had been married for seventeen years to Molly and still had to support her and their four teenage children. But Sally was upset and asked me if a prenuptial agreement meant that Clark didn't think their marriage would make it.

I explained that Clark was justifiably fearful of being vulnerable because of past losses and that the reality is that life in a relationship can mean weeks, months, or a few years. It usually doesn't really mean life. In other words, sometimes love dies. The pre-nuptial agreement does not affect the happy lifestyle you create together. It only applies to an unhappy relationship that needs to be fairly terminated. I said, "I suggest you decide whether you want to take a risk in signing away your financial rights, as well as determine how much faith you have in this marriage working. A prenuptial is of no value unless a divorce takes place. It's better for you to concentrate on keeping the marriage going rather than getting ready to be mad about a prenuptial. Your lawyer can evaluate the agreement and protect you from legal mistakes."

Cindy sent her lawyer the prenuptial agreement, and he found it fair and equitable for her and her child. She signed, and she and Clark married, and they are very happy.

In the past, culture dictated that the money a woman earned or inherited must be handed over to her husband. As long as he provided for his wife and the kids, he was a good husband. But since women's liberation freed the masculine Amazon in every woman, and the laws became more supportive of women's rights, especially in the divorce courts, getting married doesn't mean turning over money automatically. The money each person earns is his or her own. Turning it over to the marriage community must be a free, voluntary, good business decision.

The one rule I support is that the person who brings in the largest portion of the money, the masculine-energy person, whether man or woman, always has the right to determine whether to control their money, allocate control to the spouse, or have a professional do it.

Masculine-energy men and women always pay attention to their financial vulnerability and responsibilities. A masculine-energy man shows his love by taking care of his money-making career. He knows that if he slacks off in the area of money-making, he risks the loss of respect for himself. Feminine-energy women and men pay more attention to their feelings, physical well-being, vulnerability, and loss of self-controlled independence.

There cannot be two presidents in a corporation. In most marriages, the man most often brings in more money, so usually, it's the man who decides how the money is spent, as long as his wife is comfortable. If your ideal is to be the vice president or the female, then your man will be the one who structures the finances. As the female energy, you're with a man you respect. You don't compete with him or expect him to be the all-generous daddy to whom you say, "If you loved me, you'd let me do what I want.' That's immature and irresponsible.

The way a feminine-energy woman supports her hard-working masculine-energy man is by being feminine. Being a smart woman, and possibly even smarter than your man, doesn't automatically give you the right to take over the job of masculine-energy problem-solving. If you're the feminine-energy partner by choice, you voluntarily choose to defer to his leadership because he's 51 percent worth it to you. Respecting your masculine-energy man, as long as he is moral and ethical, may mean you follow him even when he may be inefficient, ineffective, and uneconomical in your masculine-energy eyes.

If you and your man are both working, you can share fifty-fifty if your incomes are nearly equal, or, you can do a percentage amount from both incomes that will cover the household money and allow each of you leftover money in your separate accounts. Or, you can put away all your combined income in a joint account and draw out stipends or allowances for pin money. Both of you can pay bills, or you can pay, or he can, or you can alternate months. As long as you have a formula that each is comfortable with, it will work. Having no formula means that one or both of you will try to control with money.

## If You're More Successful Than He Is

Sandy, 42, was promoted to vice president in charge of her division of a computer franchise. With the promotion came a significant raise, which resulted in her making twice the money her husband Bruce, 45, made. Bruce prided himself on how he paid their bills and saw to it that no late charges occurred, and money was saved and invested. They had never had hard feelings over how money came in or went out, but when Sandy told him about the raise and promotion, Bruce muttered, "I guess now you'll want to run the show." Bruce was obviously afraid she would take control, and she did wonder if she should take more interest in their money, now that she was bringing in so much.

When they came in to see me, I gave them suggestions for various ways they could handle their money issues, and they came to a new agreement. He still channeled the money, but she chose to look at the books once a month. This satisfied them both.

Having more money than your man doesn't automatically give you the right to be the masculine energy in the relationship. Men also have the right to determine how and who shall control their money in marriage. You and your man must negotiate which of you will handle your finances. It doesn't matter who writes the checks as long as one person is in charge.

Of course, problems may come along when the equation changes. If children come and one of you stops working, or if both of you are working but resources are stretched and different money priorities emerge, if you have developed a system of negotiation you'll be able to meet these problems successfully. If not, you're probably in for some difficult times. I usually tell a feminine-energy woman that her man will feel as comfortable as his career feels. And when he loses his career, or if it is shaky, or his money is mishandled, his ego gets shaken.

## When a Man Loses His Job

Bill, 30, recently laid off as a computer programmer for an aerospace company that lost a government bid, knew he would and could get a new job before his money ran out. But his wife, Gloria, 38, pregnant with their first child, was terrified. How would they make the house payments? What about their plan for a vacation before the baby came? She fantasized her life failing just as it was beginning. Gloria had chosen to be feminine in her marriage, but now she came to a seminar and asked me if roles change when a respectable husband is laid off.

I said, Yes, he must be respected even though unemployed, but you must help earn a living, which may be a role change for you from feminine energy to masculine energy. Too often a woman loses respect and sexual attraction toward an unemployed husband and becomes a righteous bitch.

If you love and respect your man during his down periods he'll work harder out of appreciation and cherishing of your love. Of course, pragmatic roles must be adjusted, such as chores around the home. If you must go outside the home to work and he has more time while unemployed, he would do well to work more at home to balance work and play. Mutate, don't eliminate. Problems arise to give you a chance to learn how to love even better, not to destroy your love.

Bill was right. Within a few months, he was employed again. In the interim, even though she was nervous, she stayed respectful. Bill appreciated her for it, and the marriage became more solid.

## Resentment at Having to Find a Second Job

Sally, 35, and Dan, 41, had always worked well together in their franchise laundry. But now, with redevelopment in their area from home to commercial property, their business was suffering. The franchise head office had told them there would be a relocation in the next year, but in the meantime, their profits would be smaller than before.

Sally knew she had to get some substitute teaching assignments during this dry spell, but she resented having to find a second job to help support the two of them, and she found playing the male role uncomfortable. She came to a seminar and asked me what she should do.

I said, "Do it if he's worth it. He's having a bad time as a respectable man today, but has he been a good man before today? Does he have credit in the respect department? In a covenant marriage, each partner helps the marriage survive even when one team member falls off for a while. You must decide if you can carry the load temporarily, or you must abandon ship."

Sally knew that Dan was more than worth it. He was a good man whom she adored. She managed to get some substitute teaching assignments and help Dan in the laundry without resentment. Five months later they relocated the business and now they are doing very well.

## If Your Masculine Man is Cheap

Sometimes, even if you, as a feminine-energy woman, follow, receive, and are available and respectful of his giving, protecting, and cherishing, you may still find your husband is stingy on one or more levels. More commonly, he'll be stingy on all levels, since generosity shows itself as an attitude behind every act.

Stingy men and women keep ledger sheets in their heads. They want 100 percent return for their giving. Equity feels like being used to them. They are usually narcissistic and selfish and want you to respect their ideas about generosity while also cherishing their feelings by not complaining about it.

You, however, a masculine-energy man or woman who's cheap may simply be conservative, looking out for the future, and may want the feminine-energy woman or man in the marriage, to respect his or her decisions. If this is your situation, and you also want respect for your ideas about how much money you should have, there are one too many masculine-energy respectable people in your marriage. Someone needs to voluntarily go back into the feminine-energy role, or be castrated verbally by the more powerful partner, and sometimes physical abuser.

Decide if you want this man as is and accept (love) him and approve of (like) his ideas enough to stay on his terms, allowing him to be respected and you to be cherished, often more so when he feels good and realizes you're willing to follow his directions. Masculine-energy men and women will be more generous, protective, and cherishing when they're respected, and less generous, protective, and cherishing when they aren't respected by women and men equal in masculine energy.

## When He Doesn't Live Up to His Commitments

Sarah, 32, and Herb, 34, had been married six years and had two little kids, four and two. In the beginning, Sarah believed in Herb, backing him in his ups and downs financially (mostly down), and trusting his word. Now she saw the truth. She knew he made empty promises and reneged on agreements they made as a couple. Added to that, he was unable to financially support both her and the children. Sarah came to a seminar and asked me if there was anything, short of separation, that she could do.

I said, "First, don't blame yourself. The problem is his. He has low self-esteem as a man. Too often, women and children let their sensitivity and intuitiveness take the blame and say, 'I must have created this result, it cannot be him, because if it is him, my world is upside down and I am afraid I cannot right it alone.' You might have believed when you married him that you could fix the damage created in his childhood, whether genetically or psychologically, but you can't. Your husband could be suffering from an imbalance in brain chemistry, which prevents his ability to be rational, even though he is a loving man. If this is his problem, he needs help."

Before you dump him for a better deal, ask him to see a psychiatrist for a checkup. If he wants to help you and the kids, he'll go to the doctor. If he doesn't, he probably is a neuropsychologically disabled man, who in my terms, follows his feminine-energy feelings rather than following his rational mind in a masculine-energy, do-well-to-feel-good-later mode. If he refuses professional help, then you must take care of yourself and leave.

## A Fun Guy

Before they married, Jerome, 33, told Patricia, his wife of six months, that he was financially well off. But after they married, whenever she'd ask him about paying the ever-mounting pile of bills, Jerome would laugh and say, "Write a check," even though he knew she didn't have the money in the bank.

Patricia realized that Jerome had lied to her and was in fact a man who managed his money unethically. Totally confused about what to do, she asked him to come to a therapy session with me to resolve the problem.

Jerome listened carefully as I told Patricia, "If Jerome is asking you to bounce checks, which is unethical, you have the right and the responsibility to say no. Respecting him as a financial leader does not mean unethical behavior. You're an individual human being before you're a married woman. You mustn't lower your standards for anyone, including a husband, mother, father, brother, sister, son, or daughter."

Jerome angrily left the session. A few months later, Patricia. divorced him. She's now happily married to a responsible man who adores her.

Too often, money becomes a vehicle of degradation rather than a source of freedom and fun. Whenever people's egos are entangled with money-power or sex-power games, they are compensating for narcissistic deprivation. Adequate people share money and sex; they don't control others with it. When finances become a power play for one or both partners, narcissism cannot be far behind.

Hershel, 52, was a self-made man. His wife Maureen, 49, had been by his side for twenty-five years of marriage. Hershel always told her to ask for what she needed and wanted, but he got angry when she asked for a paycheck or an allowance that she could count on. He would say, "No wife of mine is going to tell me what to do with the money I earn." When she did ask for something, he always demanded an explanation, and if he thought her request was foolish or extravagant, he challenged her until she became intimidated and gave up.

Maureen came to see me on the verge of divorcing him. She'd seen an attorney who told her of her right to half of their considerable estate but also asked her to see a marriage counselor before filing, as he could see they loved each other. He thought that with some down-to-earth mediating, a divorce could be avoided.

I said, "Narcissistic men want their ideas respected and their feelings cherished, without challenges, or they punish you with verbal or physical abuse, ostracism and silence, no sex, threats of leaving for other women better than you. If you're living with a masculine narcissist, you must decide to go passive and not serve him pleasures such as sex, cooking, cleaning, or companionship, until he's willing to negotiate a better deal for you financially.

"You should get an allowance weekly or biweekly or monthly. This money is yours to do with as you wish. You should get the use of a credit card up to a negotiated amount. It's up to you if you're willing to draw the line and go on strike till he's willing to talk.

"Because games are always learned in childhood and are unconscious and automatic, game-players must understand what they're doing before they can be reeducated into intimate sharing. It's easy for a man to love a docile, submissive, doormat woman who suppresses her feelings and thoughts for his sake. It's not easy for a man to cherish a verbal, individual woman who requires him to hear about issues that affect her. I only require that you respectfully confront him in the manner I've described. To put him down or yourself up isn't loving."

Maureen asked Hershel either to get his own attorney or come with her to see me. Being a smart man, he came in and negotiated her allowance.

Women need to feel good to be sexually responsive. Money wars create sex problems. Sex problems create money power plays, such as his withholding money and she overspending it when she gets it.

Lois, 30, was furious with Ed, 35. He was always working, always gone, leaving her with the 4-year-old twins, Lisa and Harry. She was bored with homemaking and childbearing, but Ed insisted she stay home with the twins. She wasn't sure if he was on an ego trip, telling his buddies about how his wife didn't have to work because he made enough money, or if he genuinely wanted her to enjoy her life with the kids. She guessed the former and vengeance was her game. Normally conservative and thrifty, she began to spend money just to spend it, reveling in the adrenaline rush. It felt as if she were slapping Ed and getting away with it.

She spent money on trendy and sometimes trashy clothes, lots of cosmetics, pampering of all types, goodies for the kids, and redoing the house to get a rise out of Ed. But Ed was happy watching her spend money, and she suffered no guilt as she spent while he worked. But then Ed changed. Suddenly, he began controlling the money she spent, without explaining why. This caused Lois, enraged, to withdraw sexually, and soon they were talking about divorce and settlements. A friend suggested they come to see me.

In our first session, I learned that Ed's business was failing. He no longer had a choice whether or not to work hard. Lois offered to go back to work to help out, but Ed flew into a rage that silenced her. It was clear that Lois and Ed were caught in the money-sex game and would stay there until they learned to communicate their individual needs, financially and intimately. Happily, they did, using my communication techniques.

## Dysfunctional Families and Problems With Friends and Children

A dysfunctional family results when we women don't say no to use and abuse of ourselves and our children. Abuse can come either from logical, warrior men who are allowed to control us without feelings, or inadequate men who love our strength yet hate us for it, and use passive-aggressive tactics to undermine us. Dysfunctional families produce codependent kids. If either you or your husband came from a dysfunctional family, you will probably not be as intimate as you could be.

Dysfunctional parents were raised by dysfunctional parents who were raised by dysfunctional parents. These families play games to avoid real feelings and intimacy. In these games, walls are erected between family members, so that a child won't feel his or her feelings or think his or her thoughts. Worst of all, the child won't exist at all, a suicide message. It takes two generations to stop a family game. As a Certified Transactional Analyst, I assist men and women in becoming conscious of their games and hopefully, ending them forever.

Intimate healthy families negotiate between members to avoid playing games. They allow children to ask for their wants and say no to what they don't want. If you want to be the first generation to break away from your family script, use Amigo Talk every day till it's comfortable. If you need more help, seek out a professional in the field of family counseling. Your children are damaged but hopefully not your grandchildren.

## Unfinished Business with Parents

"Look at the mother to see how your wife will be," goes the old adage, and Jim couldn't have felt happier when he first met Bernice, Terry's mother. She was trim, attractive, well-dressed, well-spoken, and self-employed. Jim felt sure that Bernice had been an excellent role model for Terry.

Then, almost as soon as Jim and Terry married, Bernice began calling Terry a couple of times a day. Jim got upset over these calls because Terry would stay on the phone with her mother as long as Bernice needed to talk, often interrupting something that Jim and Terry were doing, even making love, or canceling out their plans totally. No matter what Jim said, Terry would never cut the conversations short or refuse to run to her mother's apartment when told she was needed.

Jim and Terry came to see me in hopes of unraveling this menage à trois. I told Terry that she needed to deal with the unconscious games she still played with her mother. If not, she guaranteed her marriage would fail. Getting married means switching first loyalty from your parents to your new mate. My prescription for Terry was to seek out Jim's feedback and share thoughts and feelings with him. This might bring up new options, which could be frightening, but fears could be dealt with in therapy, alone, or as a family unit.

You keeping secrets will corrode the flow of energy between and your mate, and result in your remaining as a child in your parental home, unmarriageable. Do yourself a favor and start listening and talking. Once you open up and begin to talk, you can delve into issues until you see the light. You can modify your behavior lovingly, without the need for therapy or confrontation with your parents, such as cutting back on calls or visits or refusing to lend or borrow money from them. You may, however, get in touch with more painful and complex issues such as incest, molestation, and other family abuse. These issues are best dealt with in therapy before confronting the family. You and your husband or wife can determine how much can be done alone, and how much must be taken to a professional mental health specialist.

## When Your Husband Complains About His Parents

The best thing a feminine-energy woman can do when her masculine-energy husband begins to complain about his parents is to listen quietly till you are tired of listening, then use the Stroke and Stand technique. Say, "Honey, I know you're getting in touch with the pain of your issues with your parents, and I want to listen and help you. However, I'm feeling overwhelmed (pressured, pulled down, uncomfortable), now. I don't want to reject you, but I also don't want to listen to any more today. I'll talk again later. Please feel free to bring it up again."

Of course, men have feelings that need to be expressed, but your man would do better if he got permission from you before he dumped them on you. If he gets angry because you don't want to be dumped on anymore, tell him the price for pressuring you to extend yourself on behalf of his negative feelings. It's important to use "I" statements rather than "you" statements. Say something like 1) "This is turning me off and pulling me down," or 2) "I don't want to be your mother substitute or your therapist, because then I lose respect for you," or 3) "I'm not getting on with my life and chores, and your talking is going to interfere with our home and family."

If your husband and your birth family don't get along, just keep them apart. Your relationship with each is your private "I" life and doesn't have to be an "us" affair. Your husband shouldn't interfere with your relationship with your birth family unless it takes up his married "we" time with you. Your priority is your husband and marriage and kids. Your birth family ranks number two in priority if you want a great marriage. Make a good decision and cleave to your husband.

## When a Husband Puts His Mother First

Robert, 37, came from a wealthy family. His mother inherited a fortune from her father and used the money as a hook to keep her only son in line. Jane had been married to Robert for six years. At first, the money was fun and made life easy, but every year seemed to give Charlotte, her mother-in-law, more control over Jane's marriage and life.

Jane finally confronted Charlotte and asked her to stop her hurtful and coercive methods, but Charlotte refused. This conflict led to Robert growing angry at Jane, something that had been going on for over a year. Robert refused to give to her until and unless she forgave his mother. Jane came to me to ask what she should do.

I told her, "If your husband places his mother ahead of you and cherishes her feelings over yours, you are either a codependent doormat or a gold digger who needs his money so badly that she allows abuse. Give him the choice of ranking his women and see if you're number one. If you aren't, pull away, or else enjoy the money he brings in, and don't complain."

A mother-in-law should rank below you and your children. If she ranks higher and is more cherished by your husband, then your family is dysfunctional. Your husband must decide to be your man. He must leave his mother's influence and cleave to you and the kids before he cherishes or respects her.

A good mother-in-law defers to her daughter-in-law's position as her son's new woman. She joyously supports the family by appreciating her position after you and the kids. She becomes a part of your extended family but is still a part of the loving circle. She's a grandmother who doesn't compete with you as a mother. She gets permission from you and her son before she promises big gifts to the kids, to avoid the need for you to cause them pain if you choose to say no. She must release her precious son to your care and make peace with you by doing so.

## A Family Affair

Felice, 30, had never met her husband Larry's cousin Greg, 32, until the day of the family reunion picnic. When she saw him bare-chested, playing softball with the younger cousins, her heart began to pound. He felt the chemistry too, and an affair soon followed. Although they fell in love, they promised each other that they wouldn't break up the family. Felice didn't know whether to continue the relationship or end it as soon as possible, so she came to me for advice.

I said, "Polygamy is your right as a human being, but it's very masculine-energy behavior, especially for a feminine-energy woman who generally likes monogamy." Secrets usually cause so much inner turmoil for a feminine-energy woman that she can't feel good enough to do well. Masculine-energy men seem to keep secrets, with less inner turmoil than feminine-energy women, probably because they like a variety of sex partners. Possibly, their male physiological, neurological, and hormonal makeup allows them to have less inner turmoil. I tell clients, "Do whatever you want after you guesstimate the highest price you may be asked to pay."

If you can afford the family pain of dating your husband's cousin when you're found out, go ahead and continue. If you can't stop now, nothing is intrinsically wrong, but you must accept the results of your behavior. After the cat is out of the bag and the price must be paid, your mental health will be better if you previously decided it was an acceptable price for the benefits you gained in the affair. You and your boyfriend need to talk about price tags before you continue with the affair. You both have to come out of denial so you don't feel victimized if caught and asked to pay.

# Disliking Your Husband's Friend

Caroline, 31, was happily married to Tom, 35. She loved his family and friends except for Eric, his best friend, who made her skin crawl. She didn't know why she had such an intense dislike for him. He hadn't done anything to hurt her or her marriage to Tom, but still, his presence made her cringe. She asked me how to handle her reaction to their relationship.

Intense dislike of your husband's friend may be nothing more than animal sexual energy with nowhere to go. Having two Masculine-energy men around who both turn you on goes against a feminine-energy woman's natural drive to be monogamous. It can be confusing to have high energy with two Masculine-energy men. We humans are still driven by animal instincts such as nest protection. A natural reaction is to want to drive the interloper away from the nest.

Your husband has a right to his friend, and a right to share his home with the friend. If the friend has made a sexual advance toward you, then you have grounds for confrontation. If he's not overtly acting in a destructive way, then take a walk, watch TV, read a book, or go shopping while he's around. Perhaps double dating would desensitize you, as you watched him with another woman. Be aware of your reasons for intense dislike. Who or what does he remind you of? Do you need to work on yourself?

Chloe, 28, wanted her husband Greg, 31, to be nice to Harry, 29, her old friend from high school. When Greg, jealous, asked her if she and Harry had been lovers, she admitted they had, but said that there was nothing between them now but friendship. After that, Greg's jealousy got worse.

Chloe came to one of my seminars and asked me what to do to get Greg to stop being jealous. I told her, "You had sex with Harry, and that can't help making Greg jealous. Masculine-energy men can't handle the image in their mind's eye of their woman being penetrated orally, anally, and especially vaginally by another man's penis. Feminine-energy women seem to handle their man's past loves more philosophically, but masculine-energy women are as territorial sexually as any masculine-energy man, even about old loves. Jealousy, or the fear of losing someone to another, a better person than oneself, is something that everyone experiences. There's nothing abnormal about jealousy. It's what you do about it that can be abnormal."

Old lovers, lone wolves who are still single, rarely make good friends with your spouse. Old lovers who are married, or at least in long-term relationships, may bridge the gap as friends who don't threaten your spouse. Remember, old lovers can't be friends until they have new lovers.

Gerry, 30, and Dominic, 31, were best friends. Rachel, 28, married to Dominic for six months, had liked Gerry in the days when she and Dom were only girlfriend and boyfriend. But since the wedding, Gerry had been baiting, teasing, and sometimes insulting Rachel in front of Dom and also on the phone when he called and Dom wasn't home.

Puzzled, she asked me at a seminar, "How can I stop Gerry from venting anger toward me? Why doesn't he aim some at Dom?" I said, "Your husband's friend is in a love-hate relationship with you. My guess is he wants you for himself, but won't attempt a sexual affair, perhaps out of loyalty for his friend, your husband. So, he does mental war games to get an emotional high from you. Don't talk to him unless your husband is present. If your husband doesn't protect you, leave both of them and go to a movie."

## Jealousy Of Children

Tanya was sick of feeling angry and jealous as she watched her husband, Kevin, and their 12-year-old daughter, Kathryn, together. They loved each other dearly and showed it in every way, the way they looked at one another, their private jokes, secrets, teasing, and tickling. Tanya felt more like their housekeeper than his wife and her mother. Whenever she confronted Kevin, he would ignore her feelings and laugh, saying, "You're silly being jealous. You should be glad I'm so active as a dad. It takes the burden off you." Tanya came to me to get an understanding of the situation.

I told her that even though they love their daughters, many women feel jealous and resentful when their husband's first priority is his daughter, not his wife. Next to himself, a husband's priority should be his wife. Whenever a husband or wife places anyone, including a son or daughter, before their mate, the damage done to the marriage is the same as if one of them were having an affair.

The worst part is that your daughter did not voluntarily choose to be the other woman in your life. She probably has strong guilt feelings, and since she doesn't know why she has been chosen as a surrogate wife, she must guess the reason for your anger toward her. Unfortunately, her guess may call into question her very existence. She may think I'm not wanted here. I should be dead; I'm no good and my mother doesn't love me anymore. Mom is mad at me, and I hate her too, so, I'll cause trouble; Mom is jealous of me and Daddy, and I don't care. All of these statements may play in your daughter's head when she feels the tension of your jealousy and resentment. As a locked-out parent, you must refuse to blame your daughter. She had no choice and doesn't know what to do to stop what's going on.

Take a stand with your husband and say, "If I'm not your wife, I'll act like your sister until you notice." Move into another bedroom or to the couch. Don't make love with your husband and ask him to go to marriage counseling as soon as possible.

Men and women who get into Oedipal complexes that create emotional, mental, and sometimes incestuous alliances with their children were often victims of the same alliances in their childhood. It seems normal to them, and they think you are selfish. Unless you do something serious, as I suggested, your husband won't get it. If you get help from outside, you won't look like a jealous parent. You can't handle the situation alone. Someone else must help you to unravel it.

## Children's Jealousy

Kimmie, 16, looked in her mirror and saw a girl with braces on her teeth, no breasts to speak of, slight acne, and flaming red hair that went everywhere on its own. She also saw a girl who would never look like her beautiful mother, Alison, 38 and felt like a freak beside her. Alison, a loving mother, knew that Kimmie was jealous of her good looks and told her endlessly that she had looked almost identical to Kimmie at the same age, but Kimmie didn't believe her.

Alison came to see me, asking me what she could do about Kimmie's pain.

It's not uncommon for a daughter to be jealous of her mother's appearance. Jealousy is a natural human experience and only destructive when it turns to envy. A daughter's jealousy means that she wants your appearance and success. However, if she felt envy, it would mean that not only does she want what you have, but she wants to destroy what you have either physically, mentally, or emotionally.

It's good if she's able to articulate her jealousy. Talking to her about the normal stages of life from little to big, from dependent to independent, from awkward to smooth operator, from ungainly adolescent to sophisticated lady, and from poor to successful is the way parents help their children go from less than to more than. If your daughter is unattractive in some way that attracts ridicule, such as having a big nose, or being fat or skinny, having acne, being extremely shy or hostile, or displaying any antisocial behavior, get help. Being on her side and assisting her by getting medical, emotional, and mental help will lessen her pain and build a relationship between you. Modeling classes, plastic surgeons, medical aids for acne, therapy, orthodontics, and makeup sessions from your local department store are only some of the ways you can be on her side.

A parent's job is to help a child handle the pain of life, not to take the pain away or say it doesn't exist. "God made you the way you are. Live with it" is a flippant answer from a busy parent who discounts the child's pain. Take the time to talk and help. That alone will help a child "feel beautiful."

Her dad, or a male she respects, can help her by talking about what men find appealing in women. Some men are indeed attracted only to beautiful and/or successful women, but these men are inadequate little boys who hate women as human beings. Other responsible Masculine-energy men take it upon themselves to cherish all women, old or young, ugly or beautiful, smart or dumb, rich or poor. A man, especially a daddy, grandpa, brother, or uncle, has a responsibility to generously protect and cherish the women in his family, while the mom, grandma, sister, and aunt show the girl how to be a woman.

## Jealousy of Father and Son

Walter, 40, and Craig, 15, father and son, argued constantly, especially around Mabel, 42, the wife and mother. Usually, Mabel told Walter he was being overly critical of Craig, which Craig loved to hear, and which encouraged him to bait his dad just to hear his mom criticize his dad.

Inside, he knew he was wrong but the guilt did not stop him from playing his game of "Mom loves me more than she loves him." Mabel came to a parenting seminar, and I told her, "Don't get between men while they play their war games. Walk out of the room, house, car, movie, church, meeting, or wherever they are arguing, without saying a word. Your husband and son will notice that you, the audience, is gone, and all the fun of the war will be over. Only interfere if it gets violent and then call the police and let them handle it.

## How to Blend Two Families

A combination of masculine and feminine partners will help energy pump between you both as co-parents and the complementary kids you bring with you.

If it's the man who's the masculine energy, then it's his responsibility to cherish his new, feminine-energy wife's feelings about how much power he can use to co-parent her kids. She'll either feel comfortable with him as a real father, which means he has the right to discipline her kids as he sees fit, or a role-model father, who must get approval from her before he can discipline her kids. If the woman is the masculine-energy leader, she must do the same. She must find out if her feminine-energy, sensitive husband is comfortable with her as the kids' real mother or a role-model mom who must cherish his feelings by getting his permission before disciplining his kids.

The primary goal is to negotiate rights and privileges between the new parents. Once having shared respectable thoughts and cherishable feelings, they can channel communication between them as co-parenting problems arise. If you and your new husband are a good negotiating team, you can make up the house rules, chore list, curfews, grade point standards, etiquette, dress codes, and allowances, using my complementary masculine-feminine Amigo Talk. It may be rocky at first, but a good team effort will win.

Although most kids resist anything new and scary because they lack control, if you, as husband and wife, demonstrate good communication skills between yourselves, the kids will seek their own levels of interrelatedness without parental interference. The rule of thumb is, butt out unless bones are broken or blood is drawn. At the same time, listen attentively so that all the kids can speak up about anything. You can determine what is and what is not significant. It should be understandable and acceptable to you that kids snitch on one another as a way to jockey for priority. My advice is to ignore such statements as "Suzy said I was a pig," "Bobby said a bad word," or, "Jane put her wet towels in the hamper." Don't put down a child for tattling. Act only on damage to people or property. All else, ignore.

Being a parent or a role-model stepparent is an eighteen-year commitment to be consistent. Inconsistency can result in mental illness for children, whether based on poor step-parenting skills or drug or alcohol abuse. Consistency and firm boundaries produce mental health and predictability, which allow a good flow between team members in a blended family.

Sometimes, mixing two families can be the end of a good marriage. Usually, the reasons for the original divorces impact on the way a father and mother handle their children as a newly remarried couple. Men who leave their first wives and children often have excessive guilt about doing so and compensate for their guilt by spoiling, pampering, and accommodating their children's demands, no matter how unreasonable. Then, when the new stepmom tries to get her share of dad, it often creates rage in the children, who subsequently complain to dad about her interference in their relationship with him. She becomes the wicked stepmom when in truth, she's simply the neglected wife of a man with a priority problem.

Children can't be placed ahead of a mate, whether they are birth-blood children of a couple or step-children. Children need to see parents as a unit, whether they are natural parents or stepparents. When a masculine-energy man cherishes his children ahead of his new second wife, he is setting up another bad marriage. He may treat his new wife more as a girlfriend than as a stepmom for the kids. Their relationship excludes his kids as much as if he had two families. This may seem fine for stepmoms who don't want to relate to the kids, but stepmoms who do want in on this part of his life feel rejected and abandoned, and eventually cause trouble in the remarriage.

Women also can be difficult about their precious children from a previous marriage and may hold the kids too closely, thus blocking a new dad's ability to build a relationship with the step-kids. Sons especially can be difficult if they have taken the place of dad in mom's eyes. If mom was left by dad, the connection with her son can be a pseudo-marriage of sorts. If mom left dad and has been a single career mom to her kids, she may be unwilling to let anyone into her family, including her new husband. Women who have been raising kids alone often are afraid that a new husband will hurt her babies, and she'll block any situation in which a stepdad exerts authority. Eventually, stepdad either accepts that he is only a boyfriend/husband, or he rejects that role and tries to insert himself in her cozy unit with hostile results.

## Trouble Between Sons and Stepfathers

Calvin, 43, came to one of my seminars with a problem that I had heard many times before. He said, "I love my wife, but her grown son from a previous marriage always comes before me. How can I change this for the better?"

I told him, "It depends on whether you're the chief breadwinner and not merely another son to her. If she respects the life you provide for her and your son, you can use money as a vehicle in exchange for respect. If you're her other son, I suggest you not compete with blood. Enjoy the sharing with your brother and mom, may keep you. Which are you?"

Stuart never liked Susan's son, Tim, now 10. Married five years, Susan finally filed a restraining order against Stuart when she came home to find the boy locked in a closet for disobeying his order to eat his dinner. Tim had told of similar abuses, but Stuart always talked her into accepting his version of why he needed to punish the boy. Now she knew she needed to divorce him. She came to a seminar to find ways to help her and Tim handle their feelings.

There are a lot of groups, seminars, workshops, churches, and therapists ready to assist you, as well as this book and others. Look in your phone book for ads and your community college for classes for you and your kids. Go to a church that helps divorcing families. Call mental health organizations in your city and ask for a therapist. Go to Parents Without Partners in your area.

## Problems With Children From Two Families

When Fred, 46, left Linda to marry his secretary, Linda did everything she could to make the loss bearable for their daughter, Joanna, 12, despite her own grief. Two years later, married only a few months to Tom, 50, she found that Tom wanted Joanna to call him dad. However, Fred, Joanna's real dad, told her that he didn't want her to call anyone else by that name, so Joanna refused Tom's request. This hurt Tom, and he took his unhappiness out on Linda and Joanna in small, petty ways, like pretending he didn't hear them when they asked him for something they needed.

Linda asked me how she should handle the situation. I told her, "I think that your new husband is narcissistic and very feminine. It's too bad that he places his feelings ahead of your daughter's, because he could score bigger points with her by not putting her in the middle competitively. Support your daughter, and hope your husband comes to his senses. If he doesn't, you have a big decision to make about who is the masculine, loving giver, and who is the feminine receiver around your home."

Leo, 41, and Vera, 40, were engaged to be married in six months. Each had a child: Monica, 11, was Leo's, and Richard, 12, was Vera's. Both were from previous failed marriages. Vera had trouble watching Leo spoil Monica while treating Rick like a distant relative. Her jealousy was coming out as an attitude and was beginning to cause arguments and resentment. She came to a seminar to ask, "How can I avoid being jealous when he treats his kid differently from mine?"

I said, "Jealousy is a normal negative feeling generated by not having something you want. You want your husband to parent the child as he does his own. You don't want to accept that even if both kids were yours, each of you would parent each child differently."

It seems to me that every child isn't equally compatible with both parents. One parent's temperament seems to suit a child more than the other's. It's really sad when both parents favor one child. over the other. In this case, they have to try to compensate for natural attraction, often by counseling. Kids don't need identical rearing or loving. They need individual loving and rearing. Mixing two parental systems requires a foundation for rules of the house covering such issues as:

1. Equitable chore responsibilities.
2. Corporal punishment.
3. Rewards for good behavior.
4. Table and social etiquette.
5. Respectful and cherishing communication.
6. Delegation of parental powers to discipline directly the other's kid.
7. Accepting or rejecting the delegation of parental power from the other parent.
8. Remember that husband and wife rank higher than mother and father.

Put rules in writing for the bad days, so that you can discipline yourself and kids rationally, not emotionally. Negotiate outside the kids' hearing, then present the rules of behavior to them for their input. Kids like to divide and conquer new families because they want the old one back. It's us against them, and they're younger and stronger, so build your team first, and then take it to the kids. Only men and women who aren't narcissistic can form a compromising team in which their own feelings are negotiated till comfort is achieved. I advise each stepparent to make a list of requirements on critical issues:

"My" time alone with my kids; "our" time together with our kids; and "us" time with other families and relatives, including exes.

1. Negotiation: Of property, privacy, chores, and maintenance.

2. Money: Including how child support fits, or doesn't, into the family budget.

3. Play: Alone with my kids or yours, together with your kid and mine, and all of us together as a family.

Just as a married couple must negotiate time, space, money, and play, so must stepfamilies. If you maintain your independence or your irresponsible ways after putting together two families, it won't work.

## Family Council Meeting

Try having a family council meeting once a week at a regular time to air family issues. At these meetings, each member, beginning with the oldest and ending with the youngest, brings up a want or a "not want" for negotiation. Each person should be equally respected, and a sincere effort made to build a compromise agreement that helps the new blended family build family goals and traditions.

Here is my design for the Family Game:

1. The oldest member present is the moderator, seeing to it that cross-fighting is stopped and rules of order prevail.

2. Each member present (hopefully all members are present as missing members may be the ones who cause the most trouble) is allowed to ask for one thing they want in the family or say no to one thing they don't want.

3. Each issue is negotiated with respect and sensitivity. The issue must be specific, not general. You cannot negotiate abstracts, only practical issues. It must be something that can be tasted, touched, smelled, seen, or heard by the senses. Asking for love is general, and asking for hugs is specific. Asking for respect is general, asking that someone stop from taking clothes out of drawers is specific.

4. The members go around until all members say pass.

This venting of issues with each person having an equal voice and only age, not favoritism or power games, determining rank, will blend the family of opposites. The first blend is between new mom and dad, and then between parents and kids.

## Switching Roles

During the life of a marriage, masculine-energy and feminine-energy roles flex and bend and sometimes cross over, causing either a flow of mutuality and compatibility, like graceful dancers who intuitively know what their partners want, or conflict, confusion, competition, and chaos as narcissism makes a return appearance.

It only takes one person who is narcissistic to ruin the dance. Narcissistic people demand both respect and cherishing as they relax into what they call a committed marriage or relationship. They expect to resume their original independence. Being their real self is seen as their birthright. They believe that equality is paramount and every man (woman) for himself (herself) is
the law.

Switching roles also occurs during a long-term relationship as needs and situations change. The secret of good switching is communication of the desires and needs of each person today. How we can continue to grow and balance together is the problem to be solved here.

Jimmy thought he was doing the right thing when he asked Cindy, his wife, what she wanted all the time. Early on in their twenty-year marriage, she loved it when he asked her what to do, and when and how to do it. There were still times she liked having all the answers, but lately, she didn't want the leadership role. She wanted to be pampered and cared for and led by Jimmy. She wanted her lost femininity back. She came to a seminar and asked what to do. Should she tell him what she wanted, or just say what she didn't want?

I told her not to tell her husband what she wanted. Instead, she should tell him how she felt, and what she didn't want, including having to lead. When he asked her what she wanted and thought, she should decline gracefully and say, "I'll tell you what I feel about what you think and want, but I'm uncomfortable leading."

It could be that your husband believes that you like being in charge. If so, he simply needs to know that you want to be the feminine-energy partner. Of course, if you are a narcissist, you expect him to read your mind and guess what you need to have done and do it without your having to ask. You would rather do it yourself and then resent him. If this is you, use one of my tools for conflict resolution, such as Validation, to bring unspoken body language to a verbal level.

This communication tool makes clear the meaning underlying nonverbal body language that we pick up intuitively; tone of voice, facial expression, posture, and gestures. Cindy needed to flush Jimmy to a verbal level. She might say, "Jimmy, I sense you feel angry, resentful, uncomfortable. Am I right?" That way, she could avoid appearing to control him by demanding answers or actions.

She might say to him, "I believe you like me running things since you always ask me what I want to do or wait till I tell you what to do. Am I right?"

His answer will often be "Sometimes I do and sometimes I don't. It depends on how I feel." Spoken like a true narcissist. Your answer to this statement will let you know if you are a narcissist as well. If you also like to lead sometimes and expect him to lead other times, you both will end up confused.

If you want to be a masculine-energy respectable woman, you have to tell your husband what you want and check his feelings. If you want to be a feminine-energy woman, you have to tell your husband how you feel about what he wants and decide yes or no.

Validate the ground rules and don't require him to read your mind or fall into his need for you to read his mind.

He may be passive-aggressive and won't do what he knows you like, because he feels controlled by you and believes he must defend his manhood (what's left of it) against your momhood. If your husband is one of these men, try making a list of things to do and post it on the refrigerator, for whoever will do them (you or your man). In this way, he'll feel freer to give because he has freedom of choice. If he doesn't do anything, perhaps it's because he's a feminine-energy man and needs your leadership. You may have chosen a feminine-energy man to marry because you needed sweetness, sexiness, and gentleness more than you needed strength, decisiveness, and control, and now you're burning out as an independent, self-reliant, masculine-energy woman.

Being a masculine-energy individual earns a lot of respect but little cherishing. You may need to go on strike around the house rather than try to teach him to be generous, because I would prefer you to go passive instead of aggressive. If you verbally ask for what you want, and he's passive-aggressive, he'll do nothing, or worse yet, get it wrong, and you'll end up with more work to do.

Don't tell him what he should and should not do. No one, including yourself, feels good about being controlled by someone else unless he or she is a codependent zero. When you speak to him, stay with what you don't want rather than what you do, because not wanting is based on feeling bad, while wanting is based on thinking and controlling: "I don't want to do more around the house, so I'll go on strike rather than asking him to do it. If I ask, I'll end up fighting and getting my feelings hurt even more."

We women, because we can blend our feelings and thoughts more easily than men, have a better chance of molding men into more loving humans than they have of molding us into sex objects. Pam, 39, was definitely the masculine-energy person in her fourteen-year marriage to Paul, 40, exactly like her masculine-energy mom was to her feminine-energy dad. Then Pam read Getting to "I Do," and decided to stop being the masculine-energy person and the controller. Now she wanted to be the feminine-energy person. She asked me if it was still possible after all these years, and if so, how difficult the transition would be.

I said, "Yes, you can switch daily, with each situation, or depending on the needs of the day and of each person. I only ask that you ask permission before you power-drive a brilliant idea or dump an ugly feeling or criticism. Ask your masculine-energy husband for his ideas, even when you have great ones. When he feels respected, he can cherish your feelings."

Women are tough as nails inside (the animus) while men are soft (the anima). When we are also tough and controlling outside, we become totally masculine, iron-maiden torture machines. Our men are crushed by our power, especially when they're in love with us. We break their will and spirit and end up mad at them for allowing us to do it as if they could stop us.

A masculine-energy woman probably can't mellow out instantly, but she can discipline her mouth. Discipline seems, especially to autonomous, individuated, actualized, modern, narcissistic single people, a dirty word whose meaning is a loss of freedom and personal rights. "Why can't I be my total self?" they ask me. My answer is "You can be, as long as you marry someone who goes along with it unconditionally. A masculine-energy man in love wants to make you, the feminine-energy woman, happy. It may take him years to figure out you are a bottomless pit of expectations and assumptions and leave you. If your husband is your masculine-energy man, and you respect his thinking enough to feel safe under his leadership, then share feelings but don't boss him around."

## Two Drivers, Two Passengers

Stanley, 40, and Sandy, 38, had been married fifteen years when they came to a seminar together. Most of the time, there was a lot of friction in their relationship. After hearing me talk about complementary energy exchange, they realized they were often masculine energy versus masculine energy and feminine energy versus feminine energy.

Sandy decided that she wanted to be cherished more than respected, so I told her to seek out Stanley's thinking, opinions, and suggestions daily. Stanley, who wanted to be respected, was to check Sandy's feelings daily and in each situation so that a flowing, androgynous, ambisexual waltz could occur. They needed Amigo Talk.

The woman says, "Honey, what do you think about…………? Do you have any suggestions for me to do it better?"

After he makes his suggestions, he says, "Hon, do you feel good about my suggestion? Is there anything I can do or say to help you feel better about my suggestion?"

No task, career, job, skill, or talent is gender-related. That is sexism. Each man and woman can be gifted and skilled in any human endeavor, including homemaking, decorating, child-rearing, and flower growing. The only thing to decide is whose energy is best suited to do which task. If a woman is most gifted in handling money, she should do it, but like a lady. If the man is best suited. to child rearing or cooking, he should do it, but like a gentleman. Gender differences are biological but not psychological. We are all masculine and feminine-energy beings. It's how the AC-DC energy flows that's important, not which sex does which task. Decide freely. between you.

Albert, 42, lay on his back, his legs spread wide. Emma, his wife, 43, knew what that meant. "Do me!" and she didn't want to. Their eleven-year marriage had always been a "do me," and she was sick of it. Whenever she complained, he would counter with, "You don't love me anymore." Emma came to a women's group I run and asked me how to deal with her husband. I told her that a husband who lies in bed and whines "You don't love me anymore" is either the feminine energy whose need to be cherished is neglected, or he is a narcissistic man who wants both respect and cherishing. I said, "If he is a feminine-energy man, give him more love, affection, time together, and sex. If he's narcissistic, decide which you want, respect, or cherish. If cherishing, stay patiently passive and wait for him to give again, as a respectable man. Stop being the Wendy to his Peter Pan."

At a seminar, Debra Sue told us that her husband, Dennis, was passive-aggressive with the emphasis on passive. She said that nothing got done unless she continually pushed him. But she felt the strain and resented her husband.

I told her, "If you care too much about accomplishing and acquiring, your passive-aggressive feminine-energy husband will lie back like Peter Pan. You've allowed him to intimidate you out of your feminine-energy, passive nature, and into masculine-energy, problem-solving action even when that's not your feminine-energy, feel-good choice."

If you truly want to be the feminine-energy person in your marriage, simply stop being the masculine-energy. Stop caring about accomplishing and achieving. Let things fall down and then watch what happens. He'll either let them fall or he'll step in to save the day, like Clark Kent does when he needs to be Superman.

"Your husband lives in his passive, feminine-energy, Clark Kent persona because you're Superwoman, instead of staying Lois Lane. You dance to his tune even when you know it and don't want to do it. You're so afraid of losing your security-driven masculine-energy power that you don't realize that you're not negotiating for your right to be the feminine-energy partner. Instead, you submit to the games he plays to get you to be his mom, generous, protective, and cherishing his little boy self."

## Wendy and Peter Pan

When she came to see me, Julie, 50, described her marriage as a Wendy-Peter Pan relationship. During her twenty-two-year marriage to Hal, 58, she gave and gave. But now, she said, she was having a hard time giving. She said, "I think I gave too much for too long. I'm scared because I feel emotionally drained. How do I reverse this?"

I said, "When a masculine-energy person marries, he or she assumes responsibility for initiating leadership, while the feminine-energy person surrenders enough independence to follow the leader respectfully. But dear lady, is the mama, masculine-energy, Wendy in your marriage either by choice or by habit."

There are two possible reasons for this. Maybe you were raised and married at a time when the cultural belief was that your job was to emotionally support your husband so that he could do man's work making money. If you did this, he would give you social security. Or maybe you're lacking in feminine-energy self-esteem. This lack keeps you from feeling good about your lovableness, physically, mentally, and emotionally. Your motto is "I couldn't do better than my husband so I won't rock the boat." If this is the case, you cannot receive, be available to receive, or respect the one who gives, protects, and cherishes you above himself.

Possibly your husband was raised, like yourself, at a time when men were men and women were women, each having designated roles. The man was the breadwinner who could come home to the little woman who emotionally, physically, and mentally made his castle a place to rejuvenate him for the next day's work. Or possibly he's lacking in masculine-energy self-esteem. Masculine energy penetrates, acts on, and produces something, but your husband feels like an inadequate man who needs, requires, and depends on his woman to bolster him in a scary world."

I told Julie that she and Hal had set up a marriage in which she wasn't acting on her feeling good. "You're giving to him so that he feels good. You, as a giver, masculine-energy woman, are cherishing him."

I told her that if she wanted to change, she would have to do the following:

1. Communicate your feelings of being emotionally drained by using my communication technique, Androgynous Semantic Realignment WANT® Training.

2. Gradually wean your husband off your giving, protecting, and cherishing, by dropping one of your gifts per week. For example, speak up about your feelings when he orders you around. See that you don't stay up for him with a hot meal when he's late. Leave a cute note and his meal for him to heat and eat. Don't pick up his mess. Leave it till it grows moss, then throw it away or pack it all up in a box till he misses it and has to rummage.

I told her, "You know the feeling of being drained when you overextend yourself on his behalf. Jot down what caused that feeling and put it on your weaning list. At one a week, you can develop fifty-two giving habits a year. He may not like becoming a masculine-energy, giving man, but you must insist on it for your health. Over-giving, stressed-out women are susceptible to chronic illnesses such as cancer, colitis, asthma, and hypertension. I would rather you caused him some weaning pain than hurt yourself.

"Too many women in the twenty-year-marriage category would rather leave than negotiate. I'm certain that your husband loves you enough to negotiate openly and wean himself off a childlike dependency on you. Working through an imbalanced marriage is better than divorce or dying. Good luck."

## Power Games

Inadequate men and women use power games to seduce, or trick, potentially adequate partners into submission, like the rope around an elephant's leg that convinces him he cannot leave when in fact he can pull up that rope at any time. Walter, 50, was one of those men. Sara, 48, wasn't comfortable having to ask him for every penny she needed. She longed for her own money to spend on whatever she wanted. But when Sara brought up the subject, Walter's response was, "You don't need an allowance. Don't I give you everything you ask for? Within reason, of course."

Sarah was confused. Walter was a loving man and she appreciated their life, but why was it all right if their kids got an allowance but she didn't? Still, she said nothing more, reluctant to wreck either Walter's ego or their marriage. Then she came to one of my seminars and asked me what to do.

I told her that it wasn't Walter's ego she need worry about wrecking: it was his narcissistic control game. Walter's need to have total control over their money indicated to me that he felt inadequate and was afraid Sarah would find this out. Sarah's part in the game was her childlike submission to Walter. If she was ready to come out of her cocoon and be a butterfly, she would have to become conscious of painful feelings: resentment toward Walter for his playing Big Daddy; anger at herself for treating him like an authority instead of a partner, fearful of what would happen to the marriage if she became a grown-up, and guilt for the pain she would cause Walter when he became aware that she was no longer under his control. She would have to act on these negative feelings rationally, by communicating with Walter using the Cleanup technique.

She might say, "Hon, I want to talk with you about having an allowance for myself. Is it convenient to talk now, or would you rather talk later?"

He might sense her goal and attempt to filibuster her with emotions, yelling, pounding, and maybe violence. If so, she would have to stand her ground till he took time to talk, or she left either the house or the marriage and talked to a lawyer or therapist.

Walter would talk if the price was high enough, and during the talk, she might say, "I know you take good care of our family. However, I feel bad being treated like a daughter and not your partner and wife. I don't want to have to ask for every dollar I need. I would be much more comfortable and happier if I had a set allowance weekly, biweekly, or monthly. Do you think you can do this for me?"

I told her that all answers other than yes-including maybe-mean no. If she gets a yes, I suggest she gush all over him in appreciation for his being brave enough to allow her money. If he doesn't say yes, pull away quietly to whatever distance you are comfortable. Sleep in another room, like the daughter he wants you to be, or go to a hotel or stay with a friend or relative until he's willing to negotiate and stop intimidating you with his yelling, ranting, and raving.

If he's adamant about not negotiating your right to be treated like an adult partner, you should file for divorce and let your lawyer get him to agree to a full property settlement. Your husband may find that giving you an allowance is more desirable than giving you half of everything he's got. Stop enabling a bully.

## Addictions and Obsessions

Addiction relationships with high levels of pain seem like love to many. Comfort, stability, and consistency seem boring by comparison. People who are afraid of intimacy out of a fear of rejection and abandonment, and who are not health-oriented, often turn things into love objects. Food, drink, drugs, anonymous sex, money, power, and prestige become the sources of love to fill the void inside. Instant gratification seems right, although frightening, while long-term relationships seem wrong and dangerous; "Don't try to control me" has become the new motto.

Love comes in three packages: people, nature, and things. If your parents let you down when you were a child, you often turn to a dog or cat to supplement the love you need to flourish. If animals and mom and dad aren't there to share love with you, then you turn to food, cigarettes, alcohol, gambling, drugs, or worse, people, as objects to be used to gratify your needs at their expense.

Many people ask me what is fair to expect of their mates. Should they accept smoking, being overweight, lack of physical fitness, gambling, alcoholism, drugs, infidelity, or other addictions? I tell them that only they know their nonnegotiable requirements. Some people can accept these addictions in their partners, while others reject them as unacceptable. The standard is set by self-love. Whatever you feel worthy of, you will get. Whatever you don't feel worthy of, you won't get. You need to know if you cannot handle another person's addictions, whether it be booze, gambling, food, sex, work, or drugs. Either accept his or her addictions because he or she is worth it or reject him or her. Don't merely tolerate another human being.

## Infidelity

Infidelity demonstrates a lack of commitment to either self-respect or self-cherishing. Narcissists lack the ability to empathize with anyone. They respect only people who are more narcissistic than they are and who can intimidate or seduce them with fear or guilt. Power games in sex and money areas are the norm for narcissists.

Most men and women rationalize their need to be unfaithful, blaming it on their mates. "My wife is this. My husband is that. The devil made me do it." My challenge to them is always, "I hold you accountable for your decisions to respect or cherish yourself. Choose to act on your commitments to yourself or react to your partner's power over your mind and your will."

June stood up at a seminar and asked, "Why does my husband need another woman when he has me?"

My answer was "Because you let him believe he can have both and you won't leave. You are too needy. If you leave, he will get another you and add to his collection of admirers."

You can't stop your husband from having an affair. You can't stop anyone from doing anything unless you lock them up. Your husband has extramarital affairs because he's so secure that he knows he can get away with it. How many other things does your husband do that you rationalize away until the evidence hits you in the face?

Allowing him to do things that cause you pain for whatever reason tells me you either don't pay attention to your pain, or you won't set a price for his behavior because you're insecure about losing him.

If you still love him, stop sleeping with him. I don't mean only sex. Sleeping together has a lot of mommy comfort for a little boy-man. A man can get sex any time, but finding a safe, loving mommy bed isn't easy. Not sleeping together but living in the same house preserves the family, saves money, and makes your point. without the need for fighting, allows for talking things over when the urge to do so hits, and requires you to set boundaries around yourself that are good for your self-loving self-preservation.

After eight weeks, evaluate the results. Is he willing to go to counseling alone and with you? Is he still having his affair and refusing to stop? If so, you can decide if it is financially worth your while to allow him to be a brother, and come and go as he pleases, as long as he brings home the money.

If you can stay healthy during this experience, do it! He may need to get sick of himself to see how much a family means. If you can't live with him as he is, and you're deteriorating physically, mentally, and emotionally, or he's becoming violently angry and eight weeks have passed, then you must ask him to leave or leave yourself. You may need to see a lawyer to get a court order for separate maintenance and/or a restraining order to protect yourself. You don't necessarily need to start a divorce if you hope he'll clean up his act. Stay till you cannot stay any longer, then leave firmly but gracefully, like a lady.

Handle your pain by talking to your best friend, or a minister, priest, or rabbi, perhaps a counselor, or even a self-help group. Sex

Anonymous groups for wives, friends, or relations of sexaholics serve the same purpose as Alanon for wives of alcoholics. Call your local Sex Anonymous meeting and ask for directions. If this isn't available, write letters of pain, love, and pleading to your husband, but don't send them to him. Read them to your friend and throw them away. You'll feel better sharing your pain with someone.

When you talk to your husband, please remember to speak to him with respect. I believe that a woman who chooses to be a team member, primarily cherished and secondarily respected, would do well to act respectfully toward her man, even when he doesn't deserve respect but hasn't crossed the line of immoral or unethical behavior. When he crosses nonnegotiable moral lines by infidelity, drunkenness or violence, or unethical lines by gambling, fraud, or criminal behavior, she acts on the commitment to be self-cherishing by removing herself but not attacking him. He is already paying a huge price for his lack of self-respect. He doesn't benefit from your lack of self-cherishing and neither do you.

## Can You Ever Trust Him Again?

Infidelity is a sin of human frailty, not a true breach of a spiritual covenant between two people. A person who is in a covenant marriage accepts mistakes on the part of the partner as a way of demonstrating no judgmental or righteous behavior. Breached boundaries of any kind offer an opportunity to grow in your ability to love (accept) and be loved. I don't believe in trust. It seems to me trust is a hoped-for projection of perfection in another person, which is unrealistic as long as humans are human and imperfect. I like the words risk and faith better than trust.

You can't learn to trust your husband. The fact that he's a human being and therefore subject to mistakes is reason enough not to trust him to make another mistake. Instead, learn to trust yourself by taking risks, and let him build a trustworthy record that can relax your fears of abandonment and rejection. Taking a chance on him and watching his trustworthiness over time will help you have faith in your ability to love and be vulnerable to him, which will help him to cherish you more each day.

If the trustworthiness is broken and respect and cherishing are lost, one of two decisions must be made. Ask yourself whether the break is so bad you can't accept it but must leave or get sick staying; or whether you can accept this breach even though you don't approve, and build a new trustworthiness record that can, one day, earn back your respect and/or cherishing for your partner. Love is acceptance; liking is approval. You don't need to approve and like what you accept and love.

Of course, each of us has non-negotiable issues, which we may not be willing to risk once the bond is broken. Criminality, especially in the area of children or sex-violence, and betrayal may not be negotiable. Other negotiable issues can be reestablished and a new trustworthiness account begun.

Working together (in therapy is best) when things come apart is the stick-to-itiveness that demonstrates our commitment to self. He's not worth keeping a commitment to. I am if I want to love myself. Decide the risk factor of another slip, then decide if you have enough loving faith in yourself to handle it. If yes, rebuild; if not, don't. Lucille, 32, rose from the audience during a seminar and told us that she didn't trust her husband, George, 35, because she believed he had been unfaithful once before they were married six years earlier. Lucille said she kept a tight rein on George so that he would not cheat on her again. She was sure George resented her for this because he didn't call her when he was going to be late and tried to avoid her endless questions about his comings and goings.

I told her, "I believe that your keeping a tight rein on your husband because he cheated once before you were married is a more serious problem than his premarital slip. At least, making love is a natural thing humans do to bring pleasure to each other for a little while. Keeping a tight rein on him is not a loving thing to do with him; it is narcissistically cruel. You obviously believe you have the right to control him as best you can and expect him to cherish you with such things as calls when he'll be late. He can't cherish his jailor. He can only respect her out of fear."

# How Do You Forgive Someone Who Has Been Very Hurtful to You?

*You don't forgive people.* You accept them as 51 percent lovable, or you reject them as 51 percent toxic, unlovable, and unacceptable. Forgiveness is a pompous, one-upmanship game often played by religious but unspiritual people who don't know what love is. Love is accepting the unapproved, unlikable part of finite, fallible human beings, who never are or will be perfect.

Love comes in two styles: unconditional, accepting love for self and others, and conditional, approval-based love for self and others today, here and now. Spiritual, loving men and women always unconditionally love and accept themselves and others, but don't always approve or conditionally accept certain behavior. When someone does a painful thing, it's best to tell them of the pain you feel, and give them the price for a repeat performance. Keep the price minimal for the second infraction, and if there is a third crime (unacceptable disapproval of behavior), walk away emotionally, physically, and mentally, but not spiritually. Always accept the person's right to be wrong in your eyes.

Either accept them or reject them. Don't merely tolerate toxic people or you'll get sick and die early, and they won't care if you do. For love to be balanced, you must be able to freely and unconditionally accept yourself and others, and freely and conditionally reject the toxic behavior of yourself and others.

# "Why Does My Wife Want Another Man When She Has Me?"

Poor Fred. It wasn't easy for him to stand up in a seminar and ask me that question. Why was his wife in an extramarital affair with another man? Why wasn't he enough? I told Fred that for most feminine women, oxytocin bonding with a husband they are sexually happy with will keep her from acting on any polygamous desires. Therefore, a woman who wants more than one man must override her natural tendency to be monogamous. The question. is why?

'Often, women marry when they are young and sexually unsophisticated. They marry a man who's a good deal, but with whom they have no chemistry, in order to have social and financial security. Men are notorious for wanting to marry women who haven't developed sexually. An unsophisticated woman won't know that "slam bam thank you ma'am" isn't loving and affectionate but is only sex for his sake. A fully evolved woman requires lovemaking from a fully evolved man who wants more than a place to ejaculate. If a woman is married to a man to whom she isn't sexually bonded, she may negotiate a continuance of the marriage for the kids' sake. The couple may choose to remain platonic friends or sexual friends, fulfilling sexual needs without making passionate love.

If a woman married a man in order to get a daddy protector or a meal ticket, then the terms of the tab need to be renegotiated. How much money is exchanged for how much attention? Being unfaithful breaks the agreement for services rendered and is unacceptable.

If the wife is a narcissistic woman who wants more admirers, then therapy during a separation period or divorce is the only way to go. A narcissist tends to promise anything to help the status quo. It's only when you separate that the truth comes out, and she either will divorce or go into therapy to heal.

Or the wife might be a woman who can't say no to other men, and who is easily seduced as a codependent. In this case, the husband must pull back and require therapy or separation as a way to bring reality into the marriage. A codependent, insecure child-woman will helplessly ruin her life and her marriage. If this is happening, try therapy together before divorce, in order to give her the tools to defend herself against her own vulnerabilities.

A masculine man rarely can stay with an unfaithful wife. The image of her having sex with another man burns into his brain and prevents him from being in love with her. Don't tolerate unfaithfulness. Forgive and accept or reject and divorce, with love for yourself.

Another possibility you might want to think about is that your wife is having an affair out of a pathetic need to try to live a double life because of boredom. Creative sexuality requires one to use their mind to design adventures in sex play, showing that you take responsibility for seeing to it that a woman feels cherished. You must make sure she knows that you want to pleasure her and make total love to her, not just have sex for your gratification. A woman will forget that you're her husband when she doesn't feel cherished and loses respect for you and the marriage vows.

If what I've said fits you, make amends to her. Offer to seek therapy with her if she'll give you a chance and tell her to stop seeing him. If she refuses and continues to see the other man, she'll continue to bond to him monogamously. You'll be the other man because she now physically is his mate, not yours.

If you're a romantic husband who cherishes his wife's needs for creative sex, and she has simply allowed herself to binge by getting another man, her problems are deeper than your marriage. You might do well to go out and find another life partner, especially if you have children. Set up a new, loving home for them. Don't use this bad experience to lose faith in marriage and family. Have faith in yourself and take the risk again and again if necessary.

## He's a Sexaholic and She's a Co-Addict

Marilyn knew her husband, Lee, was a sex addict, constantly unfaithful to her, but she wouldn't confront him out of fear of losing him and she was sexually addicted to him. All he had to do was touch her, and she melted. But she was in pain over his infidelities. She finally came to a session with me after his most recent fling and asked whether it was a hopeless situation.

I said, "I've seen many men who have an addiction to masturbating and sex with other women. Addiction of this kind is a craving for the adrenaline high created by binging sexually on themselves or another sex object, a woman or women. These men don't like making love to someone; it's not enough passion. Passion for new conquests and new hard bodies cannot be generated in a long-term relationship. Long-termers make love to the total person, not just the sexual aspect."

If you're married to a sex addict, moving into the other bedroom will stimulate interest in you as a challenge, a contest of wills. When you're available, you're boring. Once you start pulling away, you'll be more stimulating to him. You must decide if you can live with a sex addict instead of a lover.

I suggest you be careful when he asks to swing with other couples, use drugs to stimulate higher highs or engage in a menage à trois. Don't give up your right to say no. A sex addict can't be pleased. He wants more, better, stronger sexual highs. He needs help from professionals. He may like alcoholics, overeaters, people who are bulimic and anorexic, and need medication to stop their addiction.

Your best approach is to accept him as he is today or reject him by either moving into another bedroom or getting a divorce unless he gets therapy. Again, don't tolerate him because you'll lose yourself. You can replace him, but you can't replace yourself.

All addictions are hopeless unless the addict and the co-addict look beyond gratification (him) or control (you). You can do nothing for him or to him that will help him, except let him go. If you go on to a better spiritual space, he may follow. Inspire him, don't mother him.

Two addictive people need to talk to each other in courteous ways, using my communication tools of respect and cherishing. By doing so they handle their own problems and learn to share their personal recoveries without being dependent on each other's recovery. Stay with a recovering addict but leave a rebellious, unteachable one when you see yourself slipping into your own addiction.

Kathryn, 27, came to one of my women's groups and said, "I'm having a great affair. How do I know if I should leave my husband?" I said, "By deciding if you can pay the highest guesstimated price. That may be a financial cutoff by divorce, or loss of respect and cherishing by husband, children, family, church, neighbors, or risk of being the other woman for life, or regret that your lover can never build a trust record with any wife, and he knows the same about you, and will remind you in every fight you have for the rest of your life."

Brenda, 40, was in love with two men, Frank, 45, her husband, and Jeff, 29, her best friend and lover, whom she met in an adult education class. In a seminar, she asked what to do. I told her that being in love with two people is normal for a narcissist.

Narcissistic men and women want a lover for both their masculine and feminine sides. They want one masculine-energy, hard-working, money-making, married-status-giving, stable, secure, slightly boring masculine-energy man to look up to and respect, and another person, a feminine-energy, irresponsible, feeling-centered, passionate, and free-spirited person to play with but who would not be good to marry.

"You want your husband and your best friend and lover, and you may be able to pull it off if you're a good liar, cheat, and thief. Narcissistic people can be sweet or they can be sociopathic, depending on how far they will go to get what they want. How far are you willing to go to keep two men as lovers?"

I always tell my clients that they must determine the highest price they may have to pay for doing what they are doing and be willing to pay it to be mentally healthy. If you aren't willing to pay the highest price, which in your case would be divorce and loss of both men, don't do it. Get help for yourself in making the choice.

## Alcohol

Alcohol and drug abuse create instant narcissism. All addicts are narcissistic. Alcoholics Anonymous makes it clear that all addictions are mental obsessions. When a man drinks or uses drugs, he immediately blocks his ability to think and act rationally. He frees up his feminine anima feelings and emotions, which can result in fun-loving playfulness or impulsive violence, depending on his mental health at the time. He feels a great deal like a sensitive woman who requires cherishing.

When a woman drinks or uses drugs, she immediately blocks her sensitive feelings and emotions, which tell her when to get away from dangerous people and situations. She frees up her masculine animus, which can result in conflict in her relationships, depending on her mental health at the time. She thinks a great deal like a problem-solving man, requiring respect.

A woman married to an alcoholic needs a program such as Alanon to deal with the addictive, feminine, self-gratifying men in her family. Other support systems are a Twelve-Step group, therapy, or a church counselor. The longer she enables and supports this situation, the less able she'll be to break it.

Some zero men and women don't want to get help, because they unconsciously know, or fear, that when their partner sobers up, things will be different, and maybe worse. Having an alcoholic husband allows a woman to be in control (masculine) and to feel more righteous than he is. If he were totally sober all of the time, she would lose control (masculine) and be stuck in a vulnerable position (feminine), necessitating negotiating and communicating equitably.

Harriet, 53, knew Tom, 54, had a drinking problem before she married him twenty-five years ago, but she believed that with her love and prayers, he would eventually straighten out. But the years passed, and little changed. She prayed for him daily and had their minister and doctor talk with him but to no avail. He was in and out of AA, and constantly taunted her, saying, "Get out if you can't handle my drinking. I don't need you." Now she wanted to end the marriage, but believing in her marriage vows, she felt frustrated and guilty. She asked me what she should do.

I said, "You can't make marriage vows with a drunk. If you married an alcoholic or he became one and you enabled him to stay that way all these years, you weren't married spiritually in a covenant of physical sobriety, mental compatibility, and emotional, feeling of love from your heart to his. Now, twenty-five years later, you feel trapped with your husband but you also love him. The confusion of loving and hating someone at the same time produces a victim who cannot help him or herself. You're now your husband's mother, taking care of your sick, alcoholic son, and you're hindering his recovery by using your guilt as a way to rationalize staying, based on a misguided sense of faithfulness to your marriage vows."

Decide between accepting your situation or rejecting it. Get help to break the bond, and save yourself. Stop tolerating his problems. you choose to reject his problem but not him, stop having sex, move out of the bedroom to detox yourself of oxytocin, and help clear your mind. If that doesn't get his attention, ask him to leave the home, or you leave until therapy begins. As long as his mommy is there for him he won't feel any pain.

When you get out, see what he does. Will he clean up his act or choose booze over you, his family, and his own spiritual path of love? His going to therapy, a detox center, and AA can be the beginning of a new and better life together.

Merri was sick of fighting with Bob. Alcoholic, non-supportive, passive, and belligerent, he embarrassed her in public and botched every job he had. She came to a seminar and admitted she was frightened of divorce, especially its effect on their three kids. She heard me talk of staying with your mate as long as they were 51 percent valuable. She asked how she would know if Bob was.

I said, "If being alone with children is so frightening that his alcoholism, non-supportive and passive-aggression is less frightening than being alone, stay until you can't stay, stay till being alone is better than being with him." Kids eventually grow up and leave, and so may you.

Callie, 38, pretty and in pain, came to see me about her alcoholic husband, Frank, 39, who was seeing another woman. Impulsively, she filed for divorce, but then decided she didn't want to finalize it and give him the opportunity to marry the other woman. She asked me my suggestions for letting go and also asked how she could stop feeling so sad every time he called.

I told her, "You can't stop oxytocin-bonded feelings, which are rekindled every time you speak to him on the phone. Oxytocin is a sexually stimulated hormone that nature has built into your brain to keep you in his harem. However, you need not compete with the other woman for the most generous mommy award. You need not keep your little boy alcoholic husband gratified. You can walk away like a lady who loves herself enough to require him to come home and continue the covenant marriage, not the codependent marriage."

Martin, 43, had been a periodic alcoholic, and up until four years ago, his ten-year marriage to Tricia, 38, had been happy for the most part. But in the last four years, the periods of happiness shortened to days, while the violent times during his drunken binges expanded to weeks. Tricia tried to talk to him about his drinking, but he only got more violent, once putting her in a hospital with a broken jaw. She went to Alanon and self-help classes, read self-help books, and talked to her minister, but nothing worked, so she finally left him. Now, she said, she talked to him once a week on the phone. She admitted that their conversations always gave her a rush, and she found herself upset if he called late.

Listening to Tricia, I knew that denial wasn't only his problem, it was hers. It was clear to me that their weekly phone conversation allowed Martin to get the assurance he needed that Tricia still cared about him, which allowed him to drink for another week. At the same time, she got her oxytocin fix once a week from him, so she didn't need to live with him. She had the sexual chemical reassurance that her man was still her man and not someone else's. Even if Martin was having sex with someone else, he was still in love with her. Women who stay with violent men are addicted to the oxytocin and/or adrenaline rush. I knew that neither Tricia nor Martin would sober up before they completely abstained from each other.

I said, "You must not taste, touch, smell, see, or hear him for eight weeks. He needs to feel your being gone and you need to feel the same from him. Until then you're slipping just enough to allow him to continue drinking." I advised Tricia to change the voice on the answering machine to someone else's so he can't get a fix off it and hang up if she answers when he calls. I said, "If he writes you, don't answer his letters. Walk away when he comes to the place you work. Go into the ladies' room and stay there until he leaves."

When Tricia is ready to practice sobering abstinence, she must tell Martin, "I will not be with you in any way until you are sober, in AA with a sponsor, in therapy with me, or in counseling with a minister, priest, or rabbi. I will meet with you only if your sponsor, therapist, or religious leader is present. I will not meet you alone until I am sure you are sober and intend to stay that way." Then she has to keep her word.

## Battered Women

The six months of courtship were a whirlwind of fun, dancing, and motorcycle rallies until a few weeks after the wedding, when Michael, 27, pushed Lyn, 23, to hurry up. A few days later when she didn't understand a direction, he grabbed her arm harshly, leaving a mark. A slap soon followed and eventually the arm bending, hair pulling, and eventually the punch to the stomach. Between episodes, he begged, pleaded, cried, and manipulated with controlling sex that bordered on rape, promising to stop the abuse, only to have it return more seriously. Lyn came to a seminar and asked me if she was responsible for pushing Michael's buttons. In Transactional Analysis, which is my clinical certification, we refer to three levels, or degrees, of games people power-play on one another:

1. Minor games: One-upmanship resulting in no real harm. We all play first-degree games as imperfect people.

2. Emotional and mental power games: These leave marks on the ego and soul of the other person but don't leave marks on the body. Second-degree games include verbal abuse, which undermines potency in the significant other, rendering them impotent, vulnerable, brain-washed victims of the narcissistic partner. "Battered woman" is a term for second-degree game victims who have lost their ability to stand up for themselves. Battering in the physical sense that leaves marks on the body, bruises, cuts, broken bones, hair pulled out, ligaments pulled, tissue damage, and worse, are third-degree games.

3. Second and often third-degree games: Some women come from childhood homes in which were played on them. They see these games as a normal way of life in marriage. To this type of woman, love means abuse, power, and pain. She automatically picks or is picked by an abuser to marry. She's the button she pushes on her husband. Her very existence calls for him to abuse her, especially when she has a moment of laughter joy or pleasure. This normality triggers his getting her back into submission, degradation, and fear so she can't abandon or reject him, which is his great fear. Usually, her husband or mate was also a second or third-degree victim in his childhood home, but now he relieves his impotence as a human being by marrying his

complementary victim-partner. They fit together and feel normal. Outsiders must intervene to break up the game before death does the job. Police must be called into the home by family, friends, neighbors, medical people, or religious people from a local church because the partner who batters and the partner who's battered are both unaware of their choices. They think it's normal to live this way.

I told Lyn that if she, as a battered woman, once had awareness and wasn't habituated to abuse from childhood, then she is responsible for having stayed in the relationship too long. "You let slide the little second-degree games of humiliation, first while alone with him and later in front of people. You let slide the little shove, poke, pinch, slap, until it bruised, cut, or broke you. You didn't say no, or leave, or call the police, because it seemed such a little thing, and you thought he didn't mean to do it, and he wouldn't do it again. But you were wrong, wrong, wrong.

"You pushed his animal button by not taking care of yourself as soon as possible. You either needed him, his money, status, or prestige more than you needed love, cherishing, and protection from abuse. Codependent marriages are seedbeds for verbal and/ or physical abuse. Codependent marriages are formed by immature, childlike men and women who need a 'mommy' or 'daddy' at any cost, for whatever reason. You're responsible for keeping your eyes and ears open to what's happening to you. You're responsible for staying with a man or woman whose buttons are so undisciplined and uncontrolled that you can inadvertently push them."

Domestic violence is enhanced by an addiction to oxytocin on her part and an addiction to adrenaline on his. Children raised in violently permissive homes receive a message that violence is normal. No violent TV show can do as much damage as one slap in the face of one parent by another.

Damage to children is never removed, only remediated by loving, tender consideration for this forever-wounded part. Emotional scars heal and often leave the victim stronger. "If it doesn't kill you, it will strengthen you," the old saying goes.

Carla knew when she was a child that living with Carol, her mother, and Ed, her sleazy, alcoholic stepdad with groping hands and stinking breath, was definitely not the way a child should be raised. Carla was more adult than her mother. She would be the one to drag her out of the room crying when Ed would fall down drunk, usually breaking something on the way down.

To Carla, Carol seemed hypnotized as she constantly hovered around Ed, and she never understood why. The answer came many years later, when, with my help, Carla realized that she was hovering around her own husband, Tim, when he drank too much. Although his drinking upset her, she couldn't bring herself to leave him, because it felt right to be with him. The other men she'd dated bored her. They were sober, stable guys who didn't need or challenge her. They were too nice, which seemed weak to her. She knew they each had loved her more than she loved them, and that too felt wrong. She was more comfortable with married men, drunks, and drug addicts, even though she knew better.

Carla came to see me in private sessions and learned that her mind and her body went in two directions, nice guys for her sexless brain, and bad guys for her sex-hungry body. She'd become compulsive about gratifying her body with passionate sex. The high-energy drama was her natural way of living, as opposed to living with people who gently shared love, affection, and kindness.

After Tim beat her badly in a blackout one night, Carla decided to leave him and completely abstain from him until her compulsions and addiction to him died away. She'd stayed as long as she could, more for his sake than hers, but now she had to leave and develop a taste for more normal love.

## Getting Sober

Lori, 32, a pretty woman with quick movements and restless eyes, talked about her years of addiction to drugs, alcohol, sex, and food during her marriage to her husband, George, 40.

Their marriage started with a lot of mutual love, and George was a great dad to their two young daughters, but he'd finally burnt out from being Lori's forgiving father instead of her husband. He talked her into checking into a rehab center for thirty days, as a last effort to save their five-year marriage.

Now that she was sober, on medication, and going regularly to different Twelve-Step programs, George had asked her to come back for another try. But Lori thought that George was boring and too responsible. The guys she was really attracted to were wild and crazy, and totally irresponsible. But she knew she couldn't have both her daughters and the bad boys. Lori came and told me she was confused about whether she should end her marriage or try again.

I explained to her how, during her marriage, she needed to sedate her feelings with drugs, alcohol, sex, and food. I wondered why she'd married George, and whether he was her lover or her friend. I told her that being married to a friend may be nice, but it's rarely as fulfilling as being married to a lover. I suggested she check out her reasons for thinking of going back, and talk to a counselor, religious leader, or respected relative until her head cleared. The first years of sobriety are just like a child's first years, full of curiosity, creativity, and calculated risks. Often, wives of recovering alcoholics, drug addicts, and overeaters go through their own sobering up.

Ever since Ed 35, sobered up, he hadn't seemed to show any emotion. Callie, 25, his wife, almost resented his sobriety because now he was a stick in the mud. In the past, when he drank, he was fun, crazy, and emotional. He also used to be a great lover, but now he was self-conscious and almost shy. What was the problem? Wasn't sobriety supposed to help him love and feel better? She asked him to get help, and he came to see me.

I explained to Ed that each of us, to survive a dysfunctional world, deals with our feelings and emotions differently when we disconnect them from each other through addictions. Because Ed was unable to display any emotion when he was sober, I guessed that when he drank, it was for masculine reasons. Because he released pent-up feelings while unconscious through booze, his mind forbade him from releasing them when he was sober. I advised him to stay sober and allow time to heal the chasm between mental awareness and feelings, to seek therapy to facilitate this healing, and to require Connie to respect him at this time. It's really none of Connie's business if Ed does or doesn't show emotion, as long as he cherishes her feelings by listening to her vent her pain without putting her down and asking her how he can help her feel better.

My guess is that Connie stayed with Ed during his drinking days because she had the power of righteousness. That power plays off the guilt he felt after sobering up. She could control him through his guilt, and control their home, kids, money, and decisions. But now that Ed was sober, Connie lost that power of righteousness. One way for her to get it back was to undermine Ed by picking at his defects until he went back to drinking. I told him to "Fake it till he makes it" and his body, mind, and feelings are channeled smoothly. Because Ed is willing to be helped, he'll recover. I advised him not to let criticism or stumbling discourage him on his path.

## Sweet Sabotage

Hilary, 28, a regular member of a women's self-esteem group I run, was furious. She'd recently lost thirteen pounds, and although her husband liked her new look, he soon began bringing home gifts of chocolate, which she loved. When she reminded him she was on a diet, he'd say, "Honey, you can have a treat now and then, can't you?"

Hilary saw his gift of chocolate as sabotage, a way for him to get her to go back to being a dumpy housewife, so he could stop worrying about her attracting other men. I said, "Nobody can sabotage another person intellectually unless that person is not resolved to do or not do something. You decided to lose thirteen pounds, and you acted on it. But were you dieting or were you resolved to eat differently? Dieting is a deprivation of pleasure from food strokes, but what you need is to resolve the way you love strokes from food.

As for her husband, bringing her anything nice must first be seen as a sign that he thinks of pleasing her and acts on his thoughts. I explained to her that chocolates are a gift her husband knows she likes, otherwise, she wouldn't have to lose thirteen pounds. A passive-aggressive man in the same situation might think about being nice but won't be because he feels controlled into doing something and rebels against his own ideas. The dialogue in the head of the passive-aggressive man goes something like this: "I want to be nice to her. Maybe she'd like these chocolates. I should be nice to her and buy her the chocolates. Forget it. I'm not buying her the chocolates. If she thinks I'm on the planet for her, she has another thought coming. I won't be manipulated by her. She can take care of herself, and I'll take care of myself."

I told Hilary, "If your husband's intentions are to feel secure by helping you feel insecure about your overweight body, then his intention is to sabotage you. But it doesn't matter what his intentions are. Only you can sabotage yourself. Your husband has only given you the opportunity to choose self-love or not."

Did your husband give the chocolates as a substitute for himself because he is a workaholic? If so, the chocolates are more fun and pleasure than he is, and you may eat them out of desperation. Also, think about whether you're always looking outside yourself for love and are never satisfied. There isn't enough food, drink, drugs, or sex to satisfy a self-loathing person.

Are you on a spiritual (love) path or are you still waiting for Mommy or Daddy to come and make you happy? They aren't coming in any form to fix you. You must be your own Mommy and Daddy and fix yourself. Once you become responsible and resolve to love yourself through good habits and discipline, only then can you absorb love from other humans like your husband with his chocolate love gift.

Try to see the good in everyone, but when you see bad, take care of yourself. Don't try to change your husband or anyone else. That would indicate that you believe you are their God, Mommy, or Daddy. Narcissistic people have no God. They are little tin gods. So don't you be one.

## Phone Sex, Pornography, and Peeping Toms

Men with teenage habits such as anonymous phone sex and pornography, or who are peeping toms, continue these exciting activities as a running away from adult sexual responsibilities. For this kind of man, it's easier to talk dirty to a strange sexual woman than to a good wife, and easier to look at pornography than ask his good wife to dress more sexily. He doesn't ask and escapes into a magazine or film. He can stare at other women secretly and more easily than he can lustfully stare at his good wife.

When Roberta saw the enormous telephone bills and confronted her husband, Bob, he admitted he'd been having telephone sex almost obsessively for the past month. Roberta was horrified and asked me what it meant.

I said, "First, you must accept the fact your husband probably has an addiction to anonymous fantasy sex. If you accept this, you have two choices. Either you can righteously judge him, which would probably cause him to shut down, and leave him for your own sake, or you can help him work it out.

"If you want to help him work it out, I suggest you talk to your husband about his addiction, respectfully and with love, and that you yourself bring more fantasy sex into your relationship. Set up a naughty rendezvous, as if you were having an affair, try some hot phone sex yourself, and watch adult films with him as a part of your sex life. I suggest you lighten up. Life is too short to be sexually boring. Play, as long as no one is damaged."

A man can have phone sex with a good wife, but only if she isn't set on a pedestal of superhuman ideals. Too often, we've condemned healthy men to split women into two categories: the good, virtuous, asexual, church-going woman, and the bad girl you can at least lust over by phone or in a film. The truth is, a good wife is both a Madonna to be cherished and a whore to be lusted after, and she enjoys both roles. If she doesn't, her man will often sneak around sexually, without being unfaithful or criminal.

Myrna knew her husband, Bert, had an interest in pornography, but she thought it was minor until she happened on his hidden cache of hundreds of photographs, videotapes, magazines, and books. She loved him, but what she found so totally disgusted her that she came to see me.

I said, "Your husband probably has the infantile sexuality of a thirteen-year-old. He's fixated on exploratory, anticipation sex that's passionate, exciting, kinky, irresponsible, and free for the taking. He's not mature enough to make love and build a sharing relationship. He needs to be nursed sexually. Instead of nursing at the breast like a baby, he nurses his penis, using women he thinks about, women in magazines, women on video, or any woman who can be seen as an object of gratification instead of as a human being worthy of love.

"Is his self-loving sexual play interfering with your love life with him? If not, you can see his hobby of infantile sexual practices as just that, a self-entertaining hobby. Where is it written that he needs to be an adult all the time?"

Infantile sexuality is a problem when it's illegal, such as child pornography, or peeping Tom voyeurism, or when he can't muster enough energy to make love to you after binging on masturbation. If he's a sex addict on this immature level, he likes the adrenaline rush more than making love. Sex and making love use the same genitals and result in the same orgasm, but the goal of each is different. The goal of hot sex is the gratification of the self. The goal of making love is satisfaction for both people. To love and be loved is making love and requires human sharing.

Addictions come in many forms. Watching sports on TV as an addiction is a way to avoid intimacy. A woman who's married to such a man should use the communication tools in this book, and if he refuses to negotiate, then her choices are either to accept him or reject him as an unmarriageable person. However, I don't believe in divorce as punishment for bad behavior. Such a punitive divorce generally ends up in regrets on the part of the righteous person. A good divorce is one in which attempts to fix the marriage have been to no avail and you must leave for your own sake. Apathy and empathy are signs you're ready to leave. On a small scale, you can leave and go shopping or to the theater with girlfriends. On a bigger scale, you can get a temporary separation till a successful mutual negotiation takes place or finally file for divorce. Sometimes a thump on the psychological head is needed to start an intimate conversation.

Some men cover depression with alcohol, drugs, exciting affairs, workaholism, or binge buying. Require, don't demand that he get a checkup with a psychiatrist as soon as possible, or tell him you're withdrawing from him. If you mean business and can exhibit tough love, you may be able to manipulate him into a healthier way of feeling good. If not, you need to sleep in the guest room, refuse sex, refuse to sign loan papers, and talk with a lawyer about protecting your half of the money. If you cannot get him to cherish your feelings by seeing the doctor, and if he continues to spend, you may have to divorce him. Spending your half of the money on himself is unethical and just cause.

## Midlife: When Men Become Women and Women Become Men

A midlife crisis is a natural physical, mental, and emotional event. Just about the time you believe you've learned your role in a marriage, either feminine-energy or masculine-energy, nature throws you a hormonal curveball. As time goes by, nature pushes us toward our opposite roles. Men's testosterone levels decrease, making them less aggressive and more receptive. The estrogen in their system promotes sensitivity and feeling. The masculine-energy person who used to be decisive, opinionated, and even bullheaded is now melting into a gentle soul wanting to please.

Women, however, become more actively masculine after menopause, when their estrogen level drops and progesterone impacts them more. The feminine-energy person who formerly could be led by the nose now digs in her heels and wrestles for control and self-determination. Oxytocin and estrogen call for home building and children. As they diminish during menopause, and the male hormones influence her body, a woman begins to get smarter, action-oriented, and controlling. Often, women then go out into the money world to make their mark. Some men see these women as old crows to be left and replaced by supple, nubile, younger women who extend the midlife male's idea of himself as a silver fox, a narcissistic shark man. Other men are ready to retire to their homes and pleasures such as cooking, gardening, doing some kind of artwork, and listening to music. As life goes into its apex, it follows that changes must occur. What goes up must come down, often with a bang or a flip-out.

# How to Prepare for Midlife Crises

For a couple to move through the five to ten years of midlife crises (ages 45 to 55), they must know that it's coming and prepare for it within themselves and between each other. Midlife crises mean that men or women want to take back their compromise. That compromise was made before marriage, when he chose to be the masculine-energy, respected partner, who would assume responsibility for keeping you and the kids safe and happy, sometimes at the cost of his own gratification. Your compromise was to convince you give up your right to be independent. When you have children, your body becomes their host. You cared for them for eighteen years in one way or another. Often your career was put in second place in favor of his.

To prepare for a midlife crisis, the masculine-energy man or woman should take time off to play. He or she needs to develop interests in hobbies, sports, cultural interests, and politics. Otherwise, later on, when he gets burned out from the family, new sex partners become an easier, softer way to play. Selfless masculine energy is good for half your life, then self-centered female energy must balance you, or you'll resent your loved ones as if they were a noose around your neck.

The feminine-energy woman or man should develop skills, take classes, enter the workplace, or perhaps start a business at home with a friend. Your masculine-energy man or woman needs you to lighten the load on them by emerging from your homebound status. You need to become more selfless. You must give space, consideration, kindness, and empathy to your partner's need to work less and relax more. He or she will live longer and be less likely to leave you for a less burdensome woman or man.

Talk together about your lifestyle changes. Sometimes, masculine-energy men and women feel guilty for wanting to lighten their responsibilities of making money, solving problems, and leading the family. Some feminine-energy women and men may feel put upon by being expected to work more and lead more in the relationship. These are people who act as if life came with a guarantee that they would always be cared for. With this attitude, their partners can either get sick and die from stress, or leave for a life alone with fewer responsibilities, or leave with another mate who's more willing to share responsibilities.

Negotiate modifications in time, space, money, and play during these years, so that you stay in sync with your loved one. Seek counsel from a therapist or religious counselor in your church or go on a marriage encounter weekend before you destroy your chances for a wonderful marriage to each other. These are the three stages of marriage:

1. He/she brings money and status to you, and you bring him/her, a sensuous home and a sexually available body that brings babies into the world or cares for them so she can work.

2. He/she develops his/her career to its peak, or she/he creates a sensuous, sexual home for the family.

3. After the kids are grown, and the business and money have stabilized or retirement is coming, he/she now want more leisure and fun, while you also want to balance work

with leisure and fun now that he/she is around more.

The highest divorce rate today is in the category of twenty-year marriages. Mutate, don't eliminate. Negotiate, don't abdicate. The greener pasture is usually Astroturf. Once you redesign your life together, you can feel the resurgence of energy flowing between you, but now in reverse.

Now that Glen was 60, Sally, 56, came to a seminar to find out how to handle Glen's meltdown into feminine energy, while she shifted to masculine. She wanted to know who the giver was now, and who gave back.

I told her that her husband is now becoming her wife, and she is becoming his husband. Nature sees to it that we each get to walk in the moccasins of our mates unless divorce or death intervenes. If he was a generous, protective, cherishing masculine man during your youth, now is his time of renewal and cherishing. If you were a receptive, available, and respectful feminine woman, now is your chance to make a difference in the world.

Perhaps you want more say in the money decisions, or you want to go back to school, or quit working, or pursue hobbies or interests you've put off all these years. If so, now is the time to speak up respectfully. Your husband's laughing (estrogen) gas will help him respect your ideas and wants more than when he was a young testosterone stud. He wants to have fun now and doesn't want to fight. Continue to speak respectfully and don't put him down when you ask for your wants and share your ideas. Keep him laughing so he can stay alive with you.

Ron, 62, handsome, tanned, and in great shape, had taken early retirement from his company and now spent most of his days on the golf course with his cronies. Although he was a great husband, he was no longer the lover that Cass, his wife, 60, remembered from the early marriage.

Cass, a beautiful, athletic woman, spent lots of time at the tennis courts and swimming pool and felt more desirable and sexy now than she had when the kids were at home. There was time and space for Ron and Cass to have fun sexually, but it wasn't happening. She asked me how to handle this dilemma.

I said, "Older women are like younger men-horny! Your estrogen is going down and your male hormones are impacting you more, toward assertiveness, productivity, career, and sex. When fertility is lost in menopause, nature gives us back our sex drive." However, the reverse is happening to an aging mate. He was the aggressor when you were young, but now that you're 60, you must be the seductress. Cuddle, fondle, caress, and give oral sex if you're willing, but don't disrespect him for his decline. Build his ego, because it's connected to his now feminine, receptive penis. If you want great post-60 sex, go get it. Remember, great sex is built on good memories of the last sex. Be creative, don't rely on his drive, use yours. Chase him the way he used to chase you.

## If He is Involved with a Younger Woman

When a masculine-energy man has a midlife crisis at this 20 or 30-year married mark, he sometimes decides to go backward to marriage level one with a younger woman. He thinks that she will bring back his narcissistic bachelor days, where he can stop being responsible for others' well-being and just play with his new playmate.

Here's how to handle it:

1. Don't react. Respond with acceptance. Appreciate his honest desire to be a bachelor again. Don't make him wrong or tell others what a bad guy he is. He's trying to have fun even if it looks evil to you and others. It's hard to sacrifice year after year for a family.

2. Find out who he's dating. If you can, go and talk to her or them so that they can see who you are. You may have been described as a burden rather than as a loving, attractive woman. Don't worry about his getting mad at you for seeing his girlfriend. He'll be flattered by your territoriality. Sometimes men leave for greener pastures because they don't feel appreciated or wanted except for the money and the home they provide.

3. Don't criticize the other woman. She's trying to make her life work and your husband seems right for her. Some young women spot these old war horses ready to bolt the corral as meal tickets who are vulnerable to flattery and exciting sex.

4. Don't get a divorce you don't want, no matter who tells you to do it, including your husband. Sit still and wait patiently. Midlife crises often blow over if you don't react or punish. Even if he moves in with her, sit still and wait. Get a lawyer to counsel you, but don't file for divorce unless there's a serious financial reason to do so. Too often, lawyers, once hired, get you divorced whether you like it or not, and husbands, who were only exploring separation, get fighting mad and react rashly.

5. Don't have unprotected sex with him, since he may naively believe younger women who say they are loyal and faithful,

when in fact they date married men-hardly an indicator of virtue.

Midlife narcissism can be the result of having made compromises when too young. A young man or woman who hasn't expressed himself or herself as respectable and cherishable while single, often marry prematurely, codependently, and conveniently, rather than waiting till they were true adults ready for a compromise and a covenant agreement.

Most Masculine-energy men will rebalance themselves and renegotiate the third stage of marriage with you. They often will help you pursue your career as they retire. They appreciate the money you bring to the retirement pot. You, on the other hand, can pay more attention to his sensual and sexual needs by sprucing up your body, hairstyle, makeup, and clothes.

The third marriage can be the best one but it must be renegotiated because his needs become more pleasure/oriented while becoming more productive. Time, space, money, sex, and play must be talked about with or without a marriage counselor.

## If He Buys a Young Girl Expensive Gifts

Thelma, 52, came to one of my seminars, but couldn't speak in front of the audience. Later, she came up to me and told me how humiliated she was that Hank, her 55-year-old husband, had been buying expensive gifts for their young neighbor, Daphne, who was 28 and lived in the apartment next door. Hank swore to Thelma that no sex was involved with this girl and that he loved only Thelma, and didn't want a divorce. Yet he refused to discontinue seeing his friend occasionally for lunch. Thelma asked me how she should handle this situation.

I said, "First of all, I'm glad you know about it. Secrets are more damaging than gift-giving. A 55-year-old husband could be pursuing his virility rather than his 28-year-old female friend. The fear of old age, death, and impotence can escalate into such a phobic reaction that it pushes him to act out, hopefully in nondestructive ways, such as being infatuated with a young woman and giving gifts without sex. The cliche midlife crisis covers these types of behavior.

"I suggest you listen to him compassionately talking about his thoughts and feelings. Righteousness and punitive behavior, while taking care of your fears of abandonment, will only drive him underground or away, fulfilling your projection of loss. Let his behavior be and look at the big picture of your life together. If his relationship with this young woman becomes more serious in your eyes, talk to the woman before you talk to your husband. Don't ridicule her but share your fears of loss. If she is rebellious and defiant and not a compassionate 'sister,' then talk to your husband, using my conflict tools, and set a price on the infatuation."

Don't leave him but do stop sex if you fear he's being sexual with this friend, and not just infatuated. Often a midlife crisis affair will run its course, and then he'll come home and be a better husband because he's more aware of the merits of being married to you. Aging can be devastating for some men and women. It can create symptoms of mental illness. A loving attitude often is all that's needed to live through a bad period. Accept him even if you don't approve of his behavior.

When Brent, 51, told his wife Sally, 49, he wanted to leave her to date younger women, she tried to jump out the window. Luckily, Brent pulled her back in time. The next day, she came to my office, sobbing. She told me that she loved him, and they had five kids, and asked if there was anything she could do.

I told her that a midlife crisis in a man is the time he switches from a do-good, responsible, masculine-energy man, husband, and father to a feel-good little boy who'll give up everything; wife, children, career, and home to chase a feel-good dream.

Sally's suicide attempt was dramatic and probably shocked him, but it didn't support his recovery. In fact, it may have been the final blow. Men and women in midlife crisis need patience and acceptance of their strange ways. They don't need to be punished. To them, life is slipping away without fulfillment.

I said, "Your masculine-energy husband wants to be young again. He wants to be feminine and playful. He may not have incorporated enough pleasure in his daily life, working and raising five children with you. You obviously incorporated your masculine energy, do-well side by raising this brood, and no doubt you're ready to play. But he didn't live a balanced life, and now the pendulum is swinging in a huge arc away from commitment and responsibility toward his teenage years, where he can chase younger women."

My advice is to be patient during his sabbatical leave. No matter what he does, even if he gets a young girlfriend, don't allow anyone to counsel you into starting a divorce. This is a bad piece of advice. Don't act out of embarrassment and shame because of what other people think. You can work your way through this if you're humble and patient and love him still.

If he's financially responsible, let him go on sabbatical leave till he either files for divorce or comes home. Ninety percent of these men and women do come home and settle down for the remainder of their lives. Acceptance is the way. Don't righteously reject or tolerate him. You only need to divorce if he's not responsible financially, or you find a man who wants to marry you, whom you also want to marry.

Larry, 43, told his wife Bea, 40, that although he still loved her, he needed a more exciting, butterflies-in-the-stomach kind of lover than she'd ever been. Larry felt that he'd always been dependent on a woman to be happy and now he needed space to find out who he was. He planned to move out of their home and find an apartment of his own.

Bea came to a seminar and asked if there was any hope for them, and if so, where she should go to get help. I said, "Larry wants to feel good to do well after years of doing well to feel good. He's very vulnerable to a husband snatcher at this point. There are gold-digging women waiting for well-to-do middle-aged men who want a butterflies-in-the-stomach kind of lover. These women know how to seduce men of your husband's type with sexual excitement, and there's little you can do to protect him from them."

Your best maneuvers in this situation are to check yourself for dullness, drabness, and boredom. Have you contributed to his fantasy by becoming less attractive and seductive? If so, clean up your act as soon as possible. Appeal to his eyes, not his stomach.

Middle-aged men are afraid of impotence and aging. Too often middle-aged women feel secure in their home and family and forget to give back as a sexually interesting partner. The result is that they lose it all to a second wife who knows what a man needs in order to feel good after a hard day at work or in life.

Don't tell him he's wrong for wanting to take a sabbatical leave from his marriage. You may want to ask him how you can help him find out what he wants. Does he want to move out for two months with no questions asked? Does he want to date you while he's out there? Is it okay if you socialize and date during these two months? Will safe sex be the promise?

These questions will help him feel less trapped by the marriage and will keep him seeing you as the lovable woman he once cherished. I know you won't like doing this because of your own fears, but the alternative is to block the door, causing him to fight his way out with a premature divorce. A velvet glove and a very long leash work best here. While you're waiting, first, if you learn he has already begun an affair before telling you, accept it for two more months of the therapeutic separation. Don't get righteous and don't gossip about him to family and friends. When he comes back, he will have to face them.

Second, talk to a therapist, or a religious leader, or a friend you trust.

Third, work on yourself. Entertain yourself as best you can. Don't have retaliation sex with anyone, because when your husband returns, he'll probably find out and you'll be in another problem. If he begins divorce proceedings, get the best lawyer you can afford and fight for your half of the estate. You'll need it for your life without your husband.

Fourth, if, after eight weeks, he's not closer to resolution, but you're still functioning and not getting sick physically, mentally, or emotionally, give him another eight weeks.

Fifth, beware of stress-induced illnesses. Your mind can't function in a sick body, nor can you emotionally maintain mental health. If you're deteriorating physically and need medical attention for any condition, think seriously about filing for divorce. Stay till you physically deteriorate, then abandon ship with either a separate maintenance or divorce decree. Even if you do this, there's still a chance that he'll see reality and make a firm decision one way or the other.

# Refusing to Take a Husband Back

Grace, 50, had always been taken care of by her husband, Frank, 55. They had a great traditional marriage for thirty years and raised three kids who had grown into good people. Frank had moderate success with his two print shops, where Grace helped out when needed. Then, without warning, Frank left Grace. Although his departure was abrupt, Grace later found out it was a move he had carefully planned for a year. His remarriage almost immediately after the divorce confirmed her suspicions that he'd been having an affair for a long time.

The settlement they made was fair and enough for Grace to survive on if she lived conservatively, but her big question was what to do with her life. In midlife, women and men get another chance to vote on a life path. Grace could either stagnate and dwell on her fate, or she could see this opening in her life as a fork in the road.

Grace was deeply into a two-year course as a psychiatric assistant when Frank called her up to talk. She heard his tearful remorse with detachment. She still liked him, and since the divorce, they'd had a decent friendship in spite of his hostile new wife. But Grace couldn't respond to Frank's plea to see him on the side. School was exciting, and she liked her life and friends and looked forward to building a career around helping people. Frank seemed like a lost little boy with a mean mommy who wanted to run away from his new home and back to hers. She told him of a therapist he could see, but she was finished with that part of her life.

# A Wife Who Cheated Every Ten Years

Still gorgeous at 60, Donna loved her husband, Harry, 63, after thirty years of a marriage that allowed each to be an individual, but also a good team member. They really had no outside problems. Money was plentiful, their health was great, and their kids were happily married themselves. But every ten years or so, Donna needed an affair to feel alive. At the same time, she hated herself for cheating on Harry. Now she was in a torrid affair with a 30-year-old waiter. She came to a seminar, told me her story, asked me if I thought she was weak, and wanted to know what she should do.

I said, "You're not weak. You're hungry for more, better, and different times, affection, love, or sex. It's not unusual in a long-term marriage like yours to have affairs, especially if you're a masculine-energy man or woman. Variety is the spice of life, and you've chosen to have variety rather than abort your marriage. Having an affair every ten years may not be approved of by many people, but keeping a marriage going is admirable."

Whatever is lacking in your marriage is perhaps fixable through therapy. You chose affairs as a way to handle your problems. Hating yourself isn't the goal here. Your ability to commit to a marriage through thick and thin is admirable.

Perhaps at the next ten-year mark, you might choose therapy to help you, rather than attention from another man. Flirting with another man is one type of attention. Having sex is another. Flirting doesn't produce the guilt or danger of sex but does reaffirm your attractiveness. Having sex is dangerous in many ways and still only affirms your attractiveness.

Flirt more every day to avoid affairs.

## A 59-Year-Old Baby

Gwen, 55, joked at a seminar about her 59-year-old boy-husband, Micky, who was going through his terrible twos. The audience laughed, but Gwen was serious and asked me how she could cope with his midlife crisis.

I told her to take a stand on the fact that a 59-year-old man was not a 2-year-old child in need of love, appreciation, and acceptance. Nature was pulling him out of his manhood, and he would die of a broken heart if he weren't cherished. You are given strength as you mature. You become the respectable one and he the cherishable one. Honor his previous generosity, protection, and cherishing of you and the kids by making him loved, so he can reap the loving rewards of his autumn and winter years.

Has he always been a boy-husband? If so, why have you put up with it? Was he worth it while he was young? Must he now be cast aside because he's no longer valuable? Have you awakened late to find out you never liked him, and now you're ready to dump him? Get help to answer these questions.

## A Depressed Husband Who Won't Seek Help

  Lois, 56, felt guilty for being angry at her husband, Bruce, 60. The year before, he'd contracted rheumatoid arthritis, and their life changed dramatically. He became depressed and distant and refused to see a psychiatrist. Lois empathized with him about his illness but resented his unwillingness to seek help. She came to a seminar to ask for help with this sad situation before all the love they'd had burned out.
  You can't keep your love from burning out. He's forcing you to decide if you're a mother to a rebellious, self-destructive boy, or a whole woman who can't stay unless he helps himself get better. Watch out for the tyranny of the weak. Because of the guilt you feel, they can suck the life out of you if you allow it.

## Opening the Books

  At 60, Stephanie was beginning to get frightened. Her girlfriend Mabel, 65, a widow, told her horror stories of her experiences after Hall died of a heart attack and she was thrown into a world of probate, lawyers, accountants, squabbling kids, and friends offering advice.
  Stephanie knew absolutely nothing about finances. She got an allowance from her husband, Walter, but that was it. She wasn't included in any financial matters, nor did they have a joint checking account. Walter, 63, was a good provider and loving husband of thirty years, but when she brought up the subject of money, he would brush her off, saying, "Don't worry your pretty little head about it."
  After listening to Mabel, Stephanie came to my seminar to ask me how to get her husband to open their books to her. It was clearly time for Stephanie to share her feelings about being financially ignorant, and to ask for an open-book education from her

CPA, or family lawyer, and her husband. I advised her not to rely on only her husband's information.

He might be resentful because he didn't feel respected after thirty years of being trusted. However, for Stephanie, trusting Walter at this stage of their lives could result in her being stuck with a stranger as her money manager if Walter should die before her. Strangers tend to cost lots of money. In addition, she might not be cared for as she was by Walter. "If your husband won't open the books voluntarily, then ask him if he'd rather have a bifurcated divorce. This means that either you get a property settlement through the court, which gives you your half of the money and property and allows you to remain married, or you stay business partners and get a divorce, which allows you to marry a new person."

I know how frightening it is for a woman, especially a wife of thirty years, to threaten her husband with a bifurcated divorce if he refuses to open the books before he dies. But that's what he wants, because he chose to keep secrets from you, and it's your legal right to know. In this case, you aren't disrespectful of him, you are taking care of yourself.

He may be happy to see you willing to sit down and go over everything. A good, cherishing husband doesn't want his wife to be frightened or ripped off after his death. He may be keeping business to himself because he believes you don't want to dirty your hands in it. Let him know your feelings.

Stephanie didn't have to take action. When Walter heard and understood her fears, he agreed to open the books.

## Time to Renegotiate

Gayle's hero was her husband, Paul, 56, a dynamic and successful real estate developer who now spent most of his time looking in mirrors, dyeing his hair, pulling in his stomach, and flirting with the flashy divorcee next door.

They had raised three kids well, and the last, a girl, was 20 and about to move out and live on her own. Gayle had a degree in education, which she'd used off and on in their twenty-six-year marriage. Now she was feeling bored and edgy about the prospect of days around Paul with the little they had to do. He still kept his hand on the rudder at the office, but their two sons were becoming more involved, allowing mom and dad to relax and enjoy their retirement years. Paul and Gayle needed to renegotiate this third and last phase of their marriage.

I advised Gayle to bring Paul into a postmarital negotiation of one to four sessions. He agreed, and they came in and negotiated time, space, money, and play just as any newly engaged or married couple would do. By facilitating the negotiation necessitated by midlife changes, we were able to realign their third marriage without the danger of separation and divorce.

Gayle wanted to go back to school to study music and art, which Paul agreed to. He wanted more time to play golf without feeling guilty about leaving her at home alone. Both agreed to control a certain amount of money for which they wouldn't have to account. They also agreed to look at their agreement on each anniversary and renegotiate.

Illness, loss of sexuality, financial reverses, and affairs are only some of the crises of midlife. Living life on life's terms is a wild-ride adventure. As men get in touch with their femininity (and some with their masculinity), new vistas and choices and options open up or are shut down by death wishes for peace, stability, and security. To be truly alive is to be willing to risk making mistakes and to rebuild on the lessons learned.

In midlife, we are in "geriatric puberty" with higher levels of living ahead. To remain in a stagnant adulthood would be a sad thing.

# The Rest of the Story

## Widows and Widowers

Terry came to my seminar and asked, "I'm thirty-four years old. After nine months of marriage, my wife died suddenly last month. What should I be aware of as I develop relationships with other people and foster my relationship with myself?"

I said, "Having a wife die after nine months of marriage when you are thirty-four can traumatize you and undermine your attitude toward relationships. The premature death of a loved one requires a grieving process. You mustn't rebound into another marriage unless you've done your grieving.

"How do you grieve? You talk and talk and talk, you write her letters and more letters, you may check your local churches and hospitals for grieving self-help groups, you visit her grave and talk to her. You may seek out grief therapy. You don't let your grief go underground into your subconscious, where it wreaks all kinds of damage as posttraumatic stress disorder.

"You get back into life by working, hobbies, classes, dating more than one woman, avoiding binges on sex, booze, food, and/or drugs as escapes. Take a year off to grieve before you decide to hunt for a new serious girlfriend or wife. Give yourself time to pick wisely. Life must be lived in spite of death."

At the same seminar, Betty, 64, stood up and said, "I am a widow who has been married five times. I really don't think I'm good at marriage, but I miss sex and hanging out with a man. What do you suggest I do?"

I said, "Congratulations on your five attempts at marriage. The fact that you are seeking help through this seminar indicates you're spiritually teachable. Being a widow often causes a woman not to want to go through another death. Being a divorcee is often used as an excuse not to risk marriage again and fail. Being sixty-four can also be used as an excuse not to be a dirty old lady still wanting a man, sex, and life. Go for it again."

Living alone for five years after her husband died had been lonely for Sarah, 65. Sometimes she thought it was going to be like that forever, but then Henry, 73, an attractive widower who lived next door, began dropping by for a cup of coffee and a piece of pie, and Sarah began to feel alive again. When, after a few months, Henry told her how much he cared for her and they began having a good sexual relationship, Sarah began to feel like a teenager in love.

The problem was trying to explain things to Bill, 42, and his sister, Nancy, 40, who were totally against their mom being sexually disloyal to dear dead dad. To them, being over 60 meant being sexless. It would take real independent courage for Sarah to stand up for her right as a human being to live joyously in a relationship of which her children disapproved. Sarah came to a seminar and asked me how to do it. I suggested a Stroke and Stand letter: "Dear Bill and Nancy, I know how much we all loved Dad, and I wouldn't do anything to tarnish his name. However, I love Henry, and he loves me as a woman. I don't want to be alone any longer. Henry has asked me to become engaged and I've said yes. I am having a small dinner party for a few friends and close family. Please come and rejoice with us and bless our new life. If you are too uncomfortable to give us your blessing, I will understand and sadly accept it. Love, Mother."

Happily, Sarah's children accepted her invitation, as well as accepting Henry, her future husband.

Mature men do fine as hermits and won't marry unless it feels better than being alone. Most of them develop such sensitivity that they can die in toxic, hostile environments.

Dolly, 52, a good-looking widow, owned her home free and clear, thanks to her husband, dead three years after a lingering illness. They had worked hard to raise their four kids and save for their retirement, but death ended their dream. Then, at a church bingo game, she met Jack, a 62-year-old happy-go-lucky Irishman who lived on a Social Security check. He courted her with teasing, jokes, flowers, and fun, but Dolly resisted for almost a year, out of fear of his financial instability. But Jack won her over when, on regular Wednesday night Bingo, he proposed over the microphone to the wild cheers of their friends.

Dolly came to one of my seminars and asked me whether it could work out if Jack lived with her after the wedding, and whether she could stay female even though she owned the house. I told her that, of course, she could remain female, especially if she used my techniques. Acting female may have to be an act because women who are over fifty are getting more male by the day as their estrogen levels go down. At the same time, her 62-year-old man has mellowed his assertive masculine nature physically as his testosterone level diminishes, and the estrogen in his body helps him feel more than think. Mentally, he obviously complements her energy or she wouldn't be thinking of marrying him.

Dolly's marriage to Jack had every chance of success because she was acting like a cherishable lady and not a control freak. If she remembered to pretend that Jack was still a big, strong man, he would fulfill her expectations. If, instead, she acts like a warden in her home, it won't be long till Jack either breaks out of jail or acts like a depressed jailbird.

I told Dolly that she only needs to be careful of moral and ethical situations. Her home is hers, not theirs. Her money is hers, not theirs. Of course, the same thing holds true for Jack's money and property, unless they have negotiated another agreement. She should share her home as a feminine woman, respecting her guest, and they would do fine as a couple.

# Secrets of Being a Good Wife

## 1. Choose to Be Either Respected or Cherished

You've got to know who you are before you can exchange what you've got. In every relationship, there can only be one respected masculine-energy leader and one cherished feminine-energy. follower, at least in the beginning, until a commitment has been negotiated. Choose whether you want to be the giver or the receiver, regardless of your anatomy. Whatever you choose, have integrity.

## 2. Pay Attention to Your Feelings

Avoid what you don't want. Feminine energy must feel good to do well. Masculine energy must do well to feel good. Don't rationalize away negative feelings, no matter who tells you to. If it doesn't feel good, don't do it. Honor your body.

## 3. Don't Forget the Courtship

Take care of your sexually attractive body. Aging happens to everyone, but neglect is the choice of narcissists who believe that love is blind. Men aren't blind. They need to see what they want to touch.

## 4. Learn to Communicate Your Feelings as Soon as You Have Them; Let Him Know What You Don't Want

Have the courage to speak up and don't delay by rationalizing. Men cannot read your mind or feelings. When they ask, tell them the truth in nonjudgmental, feeling-centered ways using my techniques.

## 5. Be Available And Receptive to Lovemaking At Least Once a Week

*Your body bonds to him in sex.* Neglecting your sex life is spiritually destructive. But don't ask for sex unless you have both agreed that you may. Too often masculine women with a strong need for passion ask or grab their husbands without permission, resulting in his inability to perform. Decide on your sexual style and signals. Sex is not a silent sport.

## 6. Set Aside Fifteen Minutes a Day to Talk to Each Other

Every day, you should talk, asking each other about thoughts and feelings on things that matter to both of you. Learn how to help the other to feel better and to achieve his or her goals.

## 7. Renegotiate Terms at Least Once a Year

Or whenever there is a change in your lifestyle; to give both partners the variety of switching roles. Negotiate time for I, we, us. Negotiate space for closets, drawers, den, sewing, art, and crafts. Negotiate money: mine, yours, ours. Negotiate play: nonsexual and sexual. For best results, don't negotiate lying down or while eating.

## 8. Keep All Agreements

*The only way you know you love yourself and others is by the agreements you are willing to make and keep!*

Respect and cherish each other daily. Don't give up unless he makes you sick or drives you crazy. Nobody is perfect. If he's 51 percent valuable, keep him.

## 9, Create a Romantic Memory Bank

A romantic memory is one in which the male gives pleasure to the female, and the female gives pleasure back to the male (but always a little less than she gets). Romantic memories keep him coming back for more.

## 10. Be Appreciative of and Loyal to Your Mate

Giving up your independence may mean a delay in career satisfaction, but after forty, when the kids are in school and he's more than willing to share the money burden with you, you'll be out there with the best of them. As men get older, they need more cherishing, and as women get older, they need more respect. Life comes in phases and plateaus; you don't have to have it all today. Save some for tomorrow. Your family is a gift that will keep on giving back for life. Be a good team member. Enjoy your marriage.

# Part Three

# When Nothing Works

## Separation

When negative issues stack up, often an explosion occurs that can permanently destroy a relationship. When a couple comes to my office on the verge of such an explosion, we sometimes negotiate an eight-week separation to cool things down. This therapeutic separation helps clear the air, cool the chemistry, and contributes to the processing of thoughts and feelings. It gives the couple time to renegotiate issues that were driving wedges between them.

An eight-week separation helps to stop rumination that leads to depression and illness (feel bad, think bad, feel bad, think bad, is rumination). My motto to break this back and forth between the brain and the guts is "The way out of any negative feeling is to think a positive thought and make a positive decision, and follow it with a positive action as soon as possible."

After eight weeks, both people usually can see the issues more clearly and feel the feelings more deeply, rather than being emotionally irrational. If the separation becomes more comfortable than getting back together, a divorce becomes inevitable, but at least the separation brings it on with less emotion and more logic.

Karen, 40, found out that her husband, Ray, 39, had had an affair with Sue, a business associate, on a trip overseas. Everyone in Karen's family told her that she was a wonderful wife and mother, that Ray didn't deserve her, and she should get rid of him as soon as possible. Karen and Ray did separate, but when Ray begged her to go with him to see me, Karen agreed.

In the first session, it was clear that Karen was seething with anger at Ray. Then, at my urging, she quieted down and let Ray speak. Ray told us that he did love Karen and was willing to give up Sue. That made Karen feel a little better, and they decided to continue therapy.

Over the separation period, we met to talk over the marriage issues, which for him were her weight gain, their unfulfilling sex life, and her neglect of his need for fun. Karen listened carefully and also talked about how much she hated his need to be adored by every woman he met, even if he didn't have an affair each time. Ray said he would be more careful to cherish her feelings. During their time apart, they missed each other, dated, and made love like they used to. Karen even lost ten pounds with little effort. They are back together now, much happier than they were for years. Some men resist therapy. But here's what you can do to get him into therapy before you begin divorce procedures:

• Write a sensitive letter using my Androgynous Semantic Realignment techniques.
For example:

(Paragraph 1) Stroke him (no fluffy compliments) by writing about the good parts of him and the marriage you share.
(Paragraph 2) Write about your negative feelings that have led you to separate.
(Paragraph 3) Tell him first what you don't want and then what you do want to be different in your life and marriage.
(Paragraph 4) Ask him to make an appointment with a therapist (and include the therapist's card in the letter).
(Paragraph 5) Write him about your intention to see an attorney and seek a divorce if he doesn't set up a joint visit with the therapist.

• Pack a bag for a weekend trip (Friday evening through Sunday evening). Find a friend, relative, motel, or hotel where you can stay for the weekend. Arrange for babysitters or take the kids with you.

• Quietly leave without his knowing after you put the letter where he can easily see it. In a P.S. at the bottom of the letter, tell him you'll call him at a certain time on Saturday and Sunday to see how he is and to let him know you and the kids are okay. Don't be surprised if Saturday's phone call is either angry or very sad. Don't go home till Sunday evening as planned. Sunday's call may be more loving than Saturday's.

If, when you return home, he's still full of rage and is rebellious and refuses to see a therapist, then you probably need to file for divorce on Monday. When he finds you and the kids gone, he'll feel the necessary pain of separation, which may educate him about your serious intention to take action, and what divorce feels like.

Macho-masculine men often need to get in touch with their sensitivity through pain. The above actions have a jolting effect that can stir up action before divorce proceedings begin.

If you're confused about whether to stay with your partner or leave, the Dip Stick Evaluation is a good technique that will help you make your decision. Take a small card or piece of paper that fits into your wallet, and on it mark your two choices-move out or stay. Each time one of those two thoughts crosses your conscious mind, mark your choice at that moment. Over a period of time from days to months, you'll see a record of marks that tell you how you've felt. This often stops back-and-forth rumination and helps you take action. Otherwise, you may explode into potentially dangerous compulsive behavior that you may later regret.

Vera, 26, and Pat, 35, separated after Pat had an affair with another woman. Now the affair was over, and he and Vera were trying to work things out. But Pat still talked daily to the woman on the phone, which made Vera very unhappy. She asked me, "Will it work for Pat to maintain this friendship while we are trying to work things out and possibly reunite?"

I said, "No. The other woman has a piece of his soul, which belongs to you. I believe that having genital sex is not as dangerous as having a platonic friendship with an old (or young) lover. Draw the line. You or she! Require him to place your feelings ahead of his own, or he loses you and gets to keep her if that's what he wants."

Many women ask me how they can stop loving a husband who has left them. My answer is, "You don't stop loving him. You do start living again." Of course, you'll feel bad about losing him, unless you try to drink or drug the feeling away, only to find it is still there when you sober up. But you can, as an act of will, stop love as fast as you decide to act on love for yourself. You don't need to feel good to get up, wash your face, put your clothes on, and go back into life.

A job or career can distract you, even if you don't need the money or love the work. A hobby, class, or charity commitment will occupy your mind, instead of him and the breakup. Duty dating at least once a week or going to singles events listed online or in a church bulletin is good. Letting your friends and family arrange dates for you is also a commitment to life. If you are so dysfunctional you can't live normally, then you must see your doctor or a psychiatrist for temporary medication till you "get back on the horse after the fall."

The worst thing you can do is nothing. Doing nothing allows grief to overwhelm your body and life. Reacting difunctionally to his leaving is your problem, not the problem he made for you. It isn't what happens to us that counts; it's what we do about it. Get help now. As you get back into living and self-loving, the feelings of remembered love will distill into nostalgia, which may be poignant, but not too painful. You may even end up grateful to him for leaving. Too often, people let a dead marriage go on and on. If he left appropriately, you and he have learned a lesson.

Lola had been separated from Quincy for four months. Quincy moved in with his brother. Lola was delaying divorce proceedings, hoping that Quincy would go to counseling with her to try to put their marriage back together. However, Quincy's response to her suggestion of therapy was excuses. At a seminar, she asked me what to do.

I said, "You should begin divorce proceedings. Your husband obviously isn't taking your request for therapy seriously. He's out of touch with his anima, his feminine, feel-good self. After you divorce him, he'll rue the day he refused to go to therapy with you."

## When A Man Is Afraid to Be A Wimp

Fred knew he deserved to lose Marilyn. Although he was very generous to her, he didn't cherish her feelings out of fear of being a wimp. He didn't take care of her sexual needs, and he ran from intimacy out of fear of being controlled by a woman, as he had been by his mother. His mother had always dominated him with her illnesses, sadness, and anger at his dad, and he didn't want to be controlled by feelings and emotions or illness ever again. Marilyn eventually turned to another man for her sexual needs and left Fred, which totally devastated him. He wanted her to come back and promised her he would cherish her feelings if she did. He wanted to forgive her and renegotiate their relationship. He asked me if wanting her back made him a wimp.

I told him that his willingness to forgive her indicates that he's still narcissistic. He needed to make amends to her for his part in the crisis. I said, "Don't look at her half of the game, look at yours. I like it that you're conscious of neglecting her sexually and not cherishing her feelings, and I'm sorry that she chose to replace you. "No, you aren't a wimp when you serve the needs of your woman, kids, animals, or the planet. A narcissist often acts macho, insensitive, nonintimate, and uninterested in others' ideas or feelings. A real man is secure enough to express his feminine side with compassion, humor, and empathy, especially with a woman who is secure enough to respect her man as long as he's moral and ethical. Your wife's affair indicates she didn't respect you, and you didn't cherish her out of fear that she would control you.

"You do need to renegotiate your relationship, but the problem will be that she has physically bonded to another man, and will loyally reject your offer. Continue to pursue her with cherishing behavior. Write, call, and visit. Send flowers and gifts. Make up for lost time and attention. Healthy men gain the respect of people, women, and kids by listening and negotiating deals, rather than by intimidating or seducing."

Daryl was hurt and angry. He and his wife, Harriet, had been married two years, and there was no reason to believe she wasn't as happy as he was. In fact, she'd even sent him a birthday card in which she wrote, "You are the most wonderful man in the world and I love you very much." But six months later, she left him, for reasons unknown to Daryl. When he came to see me, he said, "I'm successful, I'm old-fashioned, and I'm faithful. It's a puzzle to me how she can change her feelings as easily as changing her clothes. Why do you think she left?"

I told him that his ex-wife was narcissistic and unsuited to be on a team. My suspicion was she had a lover, or at least a fantasy lover she hoped to find. I said, "You may be too square, reliable, predictable, loving, giving, and cherishing, and she needs the excitement of the chase and the conquest. She may be back when she needs some stability and love."

Men often ask me why a woman would leave a good man for a bad one, and my answer is: because she has become sexually bonded to the other man, and her rational, self-loving mind is overwhelmed with irrational sexual obsession. Whatever her good husband did or didn't do, she didn't take the time to work through the issues with him. She either got a side-dish man so that she wouldn't have to confront her husband with her negative feelings, or she's a sexaholic who needs therapy just as an alcoholic or drug addict. She may be addicted to oxytocin. When she's sexual, she feels good, not only because she feels loved and cherished more than with her husband, but because she also feels physically good with the oxytocin. When she's not around her lover, her body starts to detox and she craves that old feeling over and over.

Stan, 31, was married eleven happy months, he thought, when his wife, Candi, 28, ran off with Mario, the man who was doing bathroom tile work in their new home. Stan was devastated. He'd thought he really knew Candi, since they'd dated four years before marrying, but now he wondered if he knew her at all. When he came to one of my seminars, he told me that after three months away, she now wanted to come back to him. He was confused about whether or not to take her back.

I said, "Take her to counseling with you. She may have overreacted to her new, good life with you and needed to sabotage it by running off with the tile man. A woman who wasn't raised by a loving daddy doesn't trust loving men later. She tends to trust and feel safe with strangers, married men who can't control and frighten her with love, security, affection, and commitment, and bad guys who abuse her.

"She may not feel worthy of a good masculine energy man or a happy married life. Her lack of femininity, feelings of being unlovable and undesirable, and of not being worthy of being cherished, indicate her lack of self-esteem. If you love her enough, take her to counseling to work things out. If not, gently and without judgment, divorce her."

## Sabotage by a Mother-In-Law

Bill knew that Charlotte, his mother-in-law, hated him from the day he eloped with her precious daughter, Sarah. Sarah was always intimidated by her mother's drive to see that she marry a doctor or lawyer, so it took all the courage she possessed to marry him, a nine-to-five worker. Bill knew they loved each other and their two kids, Sally, 4, and Sam, 2, but after he was laid off at the plant, Sarah was so insecure about her future with him, she was easy prey for Charlotte's offer to take them in "till Bill gets back to work." Sarah took the kids and left right before the Christmas holiday to punish him, he felt, for making her susceptible to Charlotte's game. He wanted to confront them and came to see me to ask how to do it.

I told him, "A mama's girl is no different from a mama's boy, except that when she leaves, she usually takes the kids with her. If your wife is an immature, unstable child-woman, and her mother is masculine and controlling, you've lost your wife and kids to a man in a woman's body."

Sons-in-law have trouble with masculine mothers-in-law unless they duel it out. I told Bill that he must confront his mother-in-law in front of his wife to let his mother-in-law know he is a better man than she is, and let his wife see him as a man in front of her masculine mom.

"At that point," I said, "she'll have to choose which masculine person she'll side with, causing her to immediately grow up. If she chooses mom, start a divorce, get a visitation schedule, and put it into operation immediately. By being decisive and firm, you'll earn the respect of both women. If you're not being confrontational and proactive, they'll know you're a feminine wimp who can't fight masculine women. Your wife needs to see you fight for her and the kids. She's obviously feminine and easily controlled by whoever takes charge.

"Be a better take-charge man than your mother-in-law. Don't hold back. Move quickly and decisively. Earn their respect even if they're mad at you. Pick up the kids for visitation and continue being a father daily. Don't badmouth their grandmother or mother. See a lawyer to begin a divorce, even though you hope things will work out before the final decree. Finally, attempt to date your wife weekly, and be courteous to her mother. Your wife may go along with mom for a while, but hopefully she is enough of an adult and mother herself to rebel at being a child again."

## When She Wants Him *and* Other Men

Larry was happy. Connie was coming home after leaving him or a year. Married twelve years, she said she would return only if he could see other men, because she needed more attention than he could give her. Larry was confused when he came to see me. Was it okay for her to see other men?

I said to Larry, "You must be a very sensitive, feminine energy nan to even be willing to ask this question. Logical, decisive, action-oriented, masculine-energy men would have slammed the door on this question and moved on to other women more willing to be monogamous. I can only conjecture that your wife was the lead of your home and you the heart, and she probably wants you to be more head than she has had to be in your marriage."

A wife's desire to have a husband and see other men is narcissistic. She wants to be with a husband because he's lovable and controllable, and nonthreatening. Dating other men on the side allows her to risk scary, respectable, controlling men till she finds the perfect balance, a respectable, decisive man who can also equally share feelings and be cherished; a fellow who rarely exists in the world of single men.

Some married men seem to be "the perfect man." They can afford to risk having a mistress because their needs are met at home. It's another thing to be a single man who's trying to build a career and share love.

If you want to explore your relationship further with your wife, you may want to accept her non-sexual relationship with other men while you do the same with other women. I call this a primary relationship. You are sexually monogamous and socially polygamous.

It's not good to live together during this period of exploration since the pain caused by other men would be a hardship for any mere mortal. If you don't date others, you won't earn her respect. She'll see you as a wimp to be controlled by her ego. If you do date others while she does, she may see you through another woman's eyes and value your sensitivity and patience more.

The key here is equity. What's good for the goose is good for the gander. If you both are narcissistic, wanting to be respected and cherished, you may commit to being a monogamous team willing to forsake all others for each other in a convenient marriage. If your wife is allowed to be a ten narcissist, while you are a zero, you haven't solved the basic problem.

Molly, 36, and Red, 37, had been separated for a year, but had recently begun talking about getting back together. She loved Red and wanted to go back to him, but knew he was having problems dealing with the indiscretions he believed she committed while they were apart. Molly wanted to help him to forgive her and trust her again and wondered if she should be up front with him and confess everything.

I said, "Only God can forgive. Humans must either accept the other as is, reject the other because of some imperfection, or tolerate the other (righteous judgment) and get sick over it, while the other goes on doing what he or she was doing without paying any price. "Don't be God. Serve God by loving yourself, and then your neighbor. Love is acceptance, liking is approval. If you love each other, you accept life on life's terms.

"While you were separated, you were free to be yourself, to explore, to experiment, to express yourself. Taking a sabbatical leave from your marriage automatically indicates you accept whatever happens, even if you don't approve. For your husband to ask what happened while you were separated indicates that he never believed you both were free to be yourselves. In his mind, you were still married, although living apart.

"Of course, you shouldn't confess anything. He can divorce you if he believes you were inappropriate, but he has no right to judge your life as if he were God or a father. He doesn't need to trust you. He needs to decide if you're worthy of the risk he may take in rejoining you in a covenant marriage. He needs to have faith in his ability to handle whatever you bring to the marriage, even the painful experiences that he may discover happened during the sabbatical leave.

"He doesn't need your confession or your apology. When he asks for evidence either to leave you, or judge and punish you, tell him, 'Honey, you have every right to ask me what I did or didn't do while we were separated. However, I'm not comfortable talking about my private life while we were apart. Do you want to accept me as I am today, or do you want to gather information with which you can get mad and leave? I'm willing to accept your leaving based on your worst nightmare of me, rather than ask for forgiveness or attempt to help you feel better about me, so you can approve of me. I'm not willing to explain, defend, grovel, or apologize for being myself and doing what I needed to do to find out more about myself."

If your loving, accepting, legal husband can't get past needing data to hang you or sanctify you, then he can't make the spiritual loving covenant. His ego is embarrassed by the awareness that other men may have been intimate with his woman. Cuckolding is embarrassing, but it still is no reason to harass you for being you. Require him to accept or reject but not tolerate you.

## Divorce

Long-term marriages or relationships must flex and grow with changing people, times, and situations. Marriage is like any business: You get out of it what you put into it. Some people believe marriages should "spontaneously" work like miracles. No! Human beings are not made of cast iron. They come in all levels of strength and endurance and have individual breaking points.

When people ask me how they should know when it's time for them to leave a relationship, I always say, "Stay until you can't stay and still be healthy in mind, body, and spirit. Don't leave your marriage unless you're physically or mentally or emotionally ill."

Each of us has a benchmark limit on toxic situations. One person can stay with a toxic mate for one year, another five, ten, or twenty-five years, but sooner or later you either get hurt by their violence, including venereal disease and battering, or your body breaks down with the stress they create because they can't or won't give up their narcissistic, selfish ways.

When violence or chronic illness occurs, you need to check the amount of abuse you are tolerating and decide whether you are willing to pay with your life. Cancer, colitis, arthritis, ulcers, high blood pressure, weight gain, and weight loss are only some of the stress-sensitive illnesses that toxic people can promote in your body if you allow it. They will live on to use and abuse another victim, who may not be able to admit his or her pain as you can and leave before dying. You can replace him, but you can't replace yourself. In the end, you may have to divorce. But even in a divorce, two people who have done all they can to communicate can know the other person's position without fear of losing power or position. The end of an intimate relationship is indicated by a sense of apathy and empathy. Apathy is the ability to think about a subject without becoming emotional. You become objective rather than subjective, so you don't personalize everything that happens. It's an unwillingness to be vulnerable to the other person's needs.

When you are apathetic, you no longer even get angry at him. When you still have anger, you still have love and are not yet finished with the relationship.

When you're empathetic, you can see that it's not you who's tearing the family apart, it's he and his uncommitted ways, and you wish he would get help from someone besides yourself. You yourself may need counseling, and if you both work toward a common goal of intimacy, you may make it.

I always say to troubled couples, "Stay together as long as you can so the lesson can be learned." Couples who abort their marriages or relationships because of psychological pain or greener-grass syndrome will inevitably repeat the same lesson in a new way next time. However, a positive divorce, like an honest bankruptcy, allows people to start over again. When life pounds people down, they owe it to themselves and their loved ones, especially the children, to start anew. You don't have to sleep in the bed you made. You can change the sheets and use prettier ones the second time around.

## Oxytocin Bonding

Some masculine energy men, after the divorce, try to talk their feminine energy ex-wives into being their friends. Don't do it. If you continue to be friends with your ex, you'll keep the chemistry going. I believe lovers cannot be friends till they have new lovers and lives. Being an oxytocin-bonded woman sets up an addiction that demands yet another fix, even during a nasty divorce or child visitation or friendly lunches, or telephone conversations. Masculine energy men can be in love with more than one woman, but feminine energy women bond to one man at a time.

The oxytocin connection is beyond the mind and beyond the will. Once begun, it makes a woman blind to another attractive man. After the divorce, the woman who's still bonded, or vulnerable to rebonding, should get away from her ex-husband's body. Don't taste, touch, smell, see, or hear him for two years, and duty-date everyone you can till you rebond to another man sexually. Compulsions are mental, and addictions are physical. Don't risk an oxytocin fix during the two years of abstinence, or while you are getting a boyfriend, because it will set you back into a chemical addiction. Only after two years, or when you're in love with a new man, can you be in touch with your ex.

## Being Sexually Addicted to One Another

John had filed for divorce. He wanted out of his marriage to Candace. They had great sexual chemistry but no compatibility. Married only a little over a year, after a rushed courtship, he knew it was right to leave, and so did she. But their great sex life continued through the divorce, and both of them were confused about how to deal with what John called their sexual addiction to each other. John came to see me to find out what he should do.

I said, "Chemistry is a body-to-body response, and it's not negotiable. It's a gift from nature bestowed on humans and animals to perpetuate the species even when partners don't like each other. Apparently, you and your wife aren't compatible, or you can't negotiate a good communication system to be compatible."

Many couples have better sex as they divorce, because they communicate about their incompatibilities more openly and with less negative energy. They finally talk to one another after years of shouting or keeping silent. If they had talked earlier as honestly as they did later, they might have stayed together. Sometimes, divorcing while still sexually attracted to one's mate turns out to be therapy that brings the couple back together. The biggest danger is the possibility of each rebounding into another marriage, with the wife staying bonded to her previous spouse, and her ex-husband still in love with her. Chaos results when the new partners discover that the sexual excitement for the old partners still exists.

If you and your wife have done everything you can, including therapy, to resolve the compatibility/ communication issues and now feel empathy and apathy for each other as life partners but the chemistry remains, there are a couple of things you can do. Because of your wife's oxytocin surges, which cause her to rebond to you over and over, you should abstain from all physical contact with her. Consciously choose to release her in spite of physical desire. If she's getting the divorce, releasing her sexually will give the marriage another chance. Even though she may be having an affair with another man to test you, the marriage, herself, or because she didn't get to be single when she was young and now wants her fling, she still belongs to you sexually. Your wife will either come back after the test and settle down, or she'll debond from you and bond to someone new, or go entirely single, but in any case she won't be physically able to have sex with you.

Many women ask me how they can break their oxytocin addiction to their ex-husbands if they have to see them because of the children. I tell them, "You don't have to see him because of the children." Stay in a bedroom while he picks up the kids. If they're big enough, have them picked up outside. Get a babysitter or a relative for an hour to make the exchange. Avoid having him come into your home, even if it is your family home, because it keeps the oxytocin bonding going. Pretend he's contagious and you must avoid him physically or you'll get sick, which will eliminate your ability to see other men as fun and possible marriage partners.

He'll probably try to intimidate you by saying something like, "This is stupid. We're still a family," or "Why are you running away?

Can't we be friends?" or "If we get along, maybe I'll drop her and come home," or "You're still my woman even if we're divorced, because you're the mother of my children," or "The kids need to see us together to feel safe." These seductive statements are meant to control you and keep you in his life and possibly his harem. Don't do it unless you like being in his harem.

Of course, if you like the harem, stop rationalizing that you can't get away, and admit you love him and take advantage of his picking up the kids or wanting to talk about the kids as a way to get a fix on him. Remember, you should not expect to be attracted to any other man, because you are still married physically to your ex. It's sometimes difficult to stay hungry for a new love while still loving and caring for the old love. Hunting requires hunger.

Even if you do get involved with someone new, being friends with your ex is bound to lead to your new love interest becoming jealous. It seems that once you have sex with someone, that person is threatening to a new love, who instinctively knows that your ex could come back and steal you away. If you do stay friends with your ex, and you're in another relationship, don't talk about your ex, take time away from your new love to deal with the ex, or place his or her needs ahead of those of the new love, no matter what the need is, whether a car, doctor, cash, or conversation on the phone while the new love waits.

If you have a friendship with an ex, keep it in your private "I" life or include your new love in the friendship by double-dating. Don't let the ex and the new lover become enemies, fighting over you and your time. Always remember who's number one and who's number two, three, and four.

If you're not yet in another relationship, get back on the horse and start dating as soon as possible. See as many different men as you can. Socialize and open yourself up to new people, but don't sexualize as a way to forget. Get your body, wardrobe, and social calendar in shape for the hunt for a new mate. In the Twelve-Step programs, the acronym HALT stands for "Don't get too hungry, too angry, too lonely, and too tired. Because when you do, you'll damage yourself by risking disabling depression, which can lead to drinking, eating too much, or illness. Move it out, don't sit on it.

## Giving Up the Anger

Leo, 45, met a young woman with an unlined face and a hard body, and left Chloe, 39, with two teenagers, both angry and sad about the divorce. Chloe saw the kids as innocent victims of their sinful father. She came to a seminar, an overweight woman with a pretty face who raged about the guilt of her husband and the pain of the children.

I said, "As long as you feel emotional about the marriage ending or about your exiting partner, it isn't over even if the divorce has been final for years. Your anger at your husband over the children appears to indicate that you assume no responsibility for the marriage's failure. However, your emotions show that you do unconsciously feel guilty for your part in the failure. Your anger at him is your way of projecting your guilt outside yourself."

Festering emotions don't continue to cause problems when filtered through the rational mind with humility. If you look inward, the result will be feelings that are rational and loving. Apathy and empathy for the bad person are signs of your own inner peace and closure. Therapy, reading about the forgiveness of self to forgive the enemy, religion, and self-help groups such as Emotions Anonymous can all help you look inside.

Try saying to yourself, "I'm going to get peace of mind back. I'm going to look inside myself and heal myself before I castigate him. I won't give my peace of mind away for any person, place, or thing." Get out of denial and defiance about your part in this divorce.

Some couples who are divorcing can't talk without fighting. This takes negotiating a nightmare. If this is you, I would advise a mediator such as a therapist, lawyer, or religious counselor. Even a professional arbitrator can be hired to assist you in resolving perceptions. Without help, emotionally divorcing couples generally are independent and self-centered narcissists, no longer willing to negotiate. They prefer intimidating with fear or seducing with guilt.

Remember, whenever there is a lot of emotion or fighting, the marriage isn't over. Hopefully, it's in passage from the pain of negative intimacy to positive intimacy in which compromise is contracted for. I suggest you mutate, don't eliminate.

Seek outside help to hear one another and make certain that the helper is for your marriage and not for a divorce. Let the divorce be the final act of your marriage, not a punishment of your partner. Punitive divorces are those in which everything possible wasn't done to save the marriage. Stay till you can't stay.

## Should Couples Go Into Therapy to Be Better Parents?

Going into therapy to be better parents means you're having a good divorce. When your former life partner is no longer that, and you are empathetic with each other and apathetic about the marriage, you can turn your eyes on the kids. Kids pay the highest price in a bad premature divorce. As the marriage disintegrates, men and women often switch to negative lovemaking, and ignore the kids or make them pawns in the game. If a couple neutralizes their emotions until they can empathize with each other and the kids, then they can begin counseling for the divorce.

Counseling can either be an autopsy of a dead marriage or a resuscitation. If by some miracle a resuscitation occurs, let it happen. Often, people decide the marriage is over and are afraid someone will revive it, so they avoid counseling. Better let whatever happens, happen. Don't bury your marriage alive.

## Conflicting Lifestyles

Larry, 26, was a vegetarian who exercised daily at certain hours. Phyllis, 25, decided she loved his lifestyle when they met in a yoga class three years earlier. She began working out with him regularly and eating nothing but vegetables. But now, after two years of marriage, Phyllis decided she hated eating only vegetables and having her exercise hours scheduled by Larry, so she stopped both practices. She was devastated when Larry told her he wanted to divorce her because she'd turned her back on his lifestyle. She came to a seminar to find out what to do.

I advise feminine energy women (and men), to follow their mates respectfully, as long as they are moral and ethical, even if he or she is inefficient, ineffective, or uneconomical.

Your husband wants you to exercise at his hour. Is there a moral or ethical reason for you to rebel against him? Would you prefer a man who respects and follows you? When a pretend feminine energy woman agrees, before marriage, to a lifestyle she really doesn't like, she often ambushes her trapped husband after the marriage, saying, "Now I don't feel like living this lifestyle, but I want you to cherish me anyway." In used-car dealerships, this is called a bait and switch.

You agreed to his lifestyle. What you do on your own is your business, as long as it is moral and ethical. If you want to enjoy a juicy steak when you're out, alone or with friends, you can do it without his permission, but don't ask him to approve of it. It isn't that you have to stop eating or drinking. What's important is that you keep agreements.

If you want to be a narcissist, both respected and cherished, one of two things will happen: either your masculine energy husband will divorce you, or he'll surrender to you and follow you respectfully. That will probably drive you away from him, all the while wondering why he couldn't please you and still be a man. Narcissism kills love.

Three years ago, Ed, 50, seemed unbearably boring to his wife, Freida, 46. She didn't feel the sexual chemistry they once had, and they separated and then divorced. But now, after three years of dating, Ed didn't look so bad. He still wanted her back, and she didn't know what to do. She'd always respected him for being a good, responsible husband, but what was she going to do about their lackluster sex life?

She came to a seminar to ask if she should go back to him, and my answer was, yes, if he looks good to you, go back to him and try. As a feminine energy woman, you need to have respect for your man and more affection than passion and chemistry, which is necessary for a masculine-energy man or woman. I usually find that if a masculine-energy man has a passion for his feminine-energy woman, and she respects him affectionately, they get along fine.

Too often, when masculine-energy women leave a good husband to find their passionate partner, they find him and he's sexy, but rarely as respectable and stable financially as their masculine-energy husband. You only get so much energy to spend between work and play. A masculine-energy man, who works hard to earn respect, needs a feminine-energy woman who'll be affectionate and available, so he can play with her at home. When a masculine-energy woman works hard, she needs a playmate. But if she doesn't want to be a career woman, she'd better stick with a masculine energy man who may not be her passion but may be her life partner. You've run away from home for three years, like a prodigal child. Go home and reward your good man with a sensuous home, a sexually available body, and lots of affection.

# Part Four

# The Rest of the Story

## Widows and Widowers

Terry came to my seminar and asked, "I'm thirty-four years old. After nine months of marriage, my wife died suddenly last month. What should I be aware of as I develop relationships with other people and foster my relationship with myself?"

I said, "Having a wife die after nine months of marriage, when you are thirty-four, can traumatize you and undermine your attitude toward relationships. The premature death of a loved one requires a grieving process. You mustn't rebound into another marriage unless you've done your grieving.

"How do you grieve? You talk and talk and talk, you write her letters and more letters, you may check your local churches and hospitals for grieving self-help groups, you visit her grave and talk to her. You may seek out grief therapy. You don't let your grief go underground into your subconscious, where it wreaks all kinds of damage such as posttraumatic stress disorder.

"You get back into life by working, hobbies, classes, dating more than one woman, avoiding binges on sex, booze, food, and/or drugs as escapes. Take a year off to grieve before you decide to hunt for a new serious girlfriend or wife. Give yourself time to pick wisely. Life must be lived in spite of death."

At the same seminar, Betty, 64, stood up and said, "I am a widow who has been married five times. I really don't think I'm good at marriage, but I miss sex and hanging out with a man. What do you suggest I do?"

I said, "Congratulations on your five attempts at marriage. The fact that you are seeking help through this seminar indicates you're spiritually teachable. Being a widow often causes a woman not to want to go through another death. Being a divorcee is often used as an excuse not to risk marriage again and fail. Being sixty-four can also be used as an excuse not to be a dirty old lady still wanting a man, sex, and life. Go for it again."

Living alone for five years after her husband died had been lonely for Sarah, 65. Sometimes she thought it was going to be like that forever, but then Henry, 73, an attractive widower who lived next door, began dropping by for a cup of coffee and a piece of pie, and Sarah began to feel alive again. When, after a few months, Henry told her how much he cared for her and they began having a good sexual relationship, Sarah began to feel like a teenager in love.

The problem was trying to explain things to Bill, 42, and his sister, Nancy, 40, who were totally against their mom being sexually disloyal to dear dead dad. To them, being over 60 meant being sexless. It would take real independent courage for Sarah to stand up for her right as a human being to live joyously in a relationship of which her children disapproved. Sarah came to a seminar and asked me how to do it. I suggested a Stroke and Stand letter: "Dear Bill and Nancy, I know how much we all loved Dad, and I wouldn't do anything to tarnish his name. However, I love Henry, and he loves me as a woman. I don't want to be alone any longer. Henry has asked me to become engaged, and I've said yes. I am having a small dinner party for a few friends and close family. Please come and rejoice with us and bless our new life. If you are too uncomfortable to give us your blessing, I will understand and sadly accept it. Love, Mother." Happily, Sarah's children accepted her invitation, as well as accepting Henry, her future husband.

Mature men do fine as hermits and won't marry unless it feels better than being alone. Most of them develop such sensitivity that they can die in toxic, hostile environments.

Dolly, 52, a good-looking widow, owned her home free and clear, thanks to her husband, dead three years after a lingering illness. They had worked hard to raise their four kids and save for their retirement, but death ended their dream. Then, at a church bingo game, she met Jack, a 62-year-old happy-go-lucky Irishman who lived on a Social Security check. He courted her with teasing, jokes, flowers, and fun, but Dolly resisted for almost a year, out of fear of his financial instability. But Jack won her over when, on regular

Wednesday night Bingo, he proposed over the microphone to the wild cheers of their friends.

Dolly came to one of my seminars and asked me whether it could work out if Jack lived with her after the wedding, and whether she could stay female even though she owned the house. I told her that, of course, she could remain female, especially if she used my techniques. Acting female may have to be an act, because women who are over fifty are getting more male by the day as their estrogen levels go down. At the same time, her 62-year-old man has mellowed his assertive masculine nature physically as his testosterone level diminishes, and the estrogen in his body helps him feel more than think. Mentally, he obviously complements her energy, or she wouldn't be thinking of marrying him.

Dolly's marriage to Jack had every chance of success because she was acting like a cherishable lady and not a control freak. If she remembered to pretend that Jack was still a big, strong man, he would fulfill her expectations. If, instead, she acts like a warden in her home, it won't be long before Jack either breaks out of jail or acts like a depressed jailbird.

I told Dolly that she only needs to be careful of moral and ethical situations. Her home is hers, not theirs. Her money is hers, not theirs. Of course, the same thing holds true for Jack's money and property, unless they have negotiated another agreement. She should share her home as a feminine woman, respecting her guest, and they would do fine as a couple.

# Ten Secrets to Staying Married

## 1. Choose to Be Either Respected or Cherished

You've got to know who you are before you can exchange what you've got. In every relationship, there can only be one respected masculine energy leader and one cherished feminine energy. follower, at least in the beginning, until a commitment has been negotiated. Choose whether you want to be the giver or the receiver, regardless of your anatomy. Whatever you choose, have integrity.

## 2. Pay Attention to Your Feelings

Avoid what you don't want. Feminine energy must feel good to do well. Masculine energy must do well to feel good. Don't rationalize away negative feelings, no matter who tells you to. If it doesn't feel good, don't do it. Honor your body.

## 3. Don't Forget the Courtship

Take care of your sexually attractive body. Aging happens to everyone, but neglect is the choice of narcissists who believe that love is blind. Men aren't blind. They need to see what they want to touch.

## 4. Learn to Communicate Your Feelings as Soon as You Have Them; Let Him Know What You *Don't* Want

Have the courage to speak up and don't delay by rationalizing. Men cannot read your mind or feelings. When they ask, tell them the truth in nonjudgmental, feeling-centered ways using my techniques.

## 5. Be Available and Receptive to Lovemaking at Least Once a Week

*Your body bonds to him in sex.* Neglecting your sex life is spiritually destructive. But don't ask for sex unless you have both agreed that you may. Too often, masculine women with a strong need for passion ask or grab their husbands without permission, resulting in his inability to perform. Decide on your sexual style and signals. Sex is not a silent sport.

## 6. Set Aside Fifteen Minutes a Day to Talk to Each Other

Every day, you should talk, asking each other about thoughts and feelings on things that matter to both of you. Learn how to help the other feel better and to achieve his or her goals.

## 7. Renegotiate Terms at Least Once a Year

Whenever there is a change in your lifestyle, allow both partners to switch roles. Negotiate these as they come up in the four categories: (a) Time; my time, your time, our time; (b) Space; (mine, yours, ours), home office, closets, drawers; (c) Money; mine, yours, ours; (d) Play; nonsexual and sexual. For best results, don't negotiate in bed or while eating.

## 8. Keep All Agreements

The only way you know you love yourself and others is by the agreements you are willing to make and keep. Respect and cherish each other daily. Don't give up unless he makes you sick or drives you crazy. Nobody is perfect. If he's 51 percent valuable, keep him.

## 9. Create a Romantic Memory Bank

A romantic memory is one in which the male gives pleasure to the female, and the female gives pleasure back to the male (but always a little less than she gets). Romantic memories keep him coming back for more.

## 10. Be Appreciative of and Loyal to Your Mate

Giving up your independence may mean a delay in career satisfaction, but after forty, when the kids are in school and he's more than willing to share the money burden with you, you'll be out there with the best of them. As men get older, they need more cherishing, and as women get older, they need more respect. Life comes in phases and plateaus; you don't have to have it all today. Save some for tomorrow. Your family is a gift that will keep on giving back for life. Be a good team member. Enjoy your marriage.

www.ingramcontent.com/pod-product-compliance
Lightning Source LLC
LaVergne TN
LVHW061035070526
838201LV00073B/5037